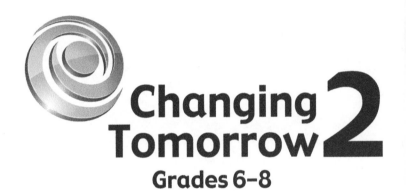

Changing Tomorrow 2
Grades 6–8

Grades 6–8

Changing Tomorrow 2

Leadership Curriculum for High–Ability Middle School Students

Joyce VanTassel–Baska, Ed.D.,
& Linda D. Avery, Ph.D.

Routledge
Taylor & Francis Group

NEW YORK AND LONDON

First published in 2013 by Prufrock Press Inc.

Published in 2021 by Routledge
605 Third Avenue, New York, NY 10017
2 Park Square, Milton Park, Abingdon, Oxon OX14 4RN

Routledge is an imprint of the Taylor & Francis Group, an informa business.

Copyright ©2013 Taylor & Francis Group.

Production design by Raquel Trevino

ISBN-13: 978-1-0321-4183-1 (hbk)
ISBN-13: 978-1-5936-3954-9 (pbk)

DOI:10.4324/9781003233619

Table of Contents

Part I: Introduction to the Unit

Part II: Pre- and Postassessments and Rubric

Part III: Lessons

Part IV: Appendices

Part I
Introduction to the Unit

DOI:10.4324/9781003233619-1

Introduction
and Overview of the Unit

Rationale

The current clarion call in education to prepare students for the 21st century is an incentive to rethink elements of the curriculum that will best serve the interests of academically gifted and talented learners. One important component of a well-rounded curriculum is the inclusion of a formalized leadership development initiative to ensure these young people acquire the knowledge and skills essential to assuming leadership roles and to practice the habits of mind that will enable them to apply these behaviors in a conscientious and compassionate way. Incorporating such instructional opportunities into the curriculum offerings takes both planning and practice.

Changing Tomorrow 2 is designed to draw on some of the most powerful ideas associated with the newest paradigm in leadership development and to help teachers incorporate this knowledge into their curricula for high-ability students at the middle school level. Although all learners can benefit from the information and exercises included here, the pacing of the lessons, the emphasis on conceptual thinking skills, and the focus on independent biographical research are best targeted to the abilities and needs of the advanced learner.

The design of the unit incorporates three conceptual strands:

- ◎ *Biographical studies*: The unit uses the biographies of seven leaders drawn from a cross-section of fields to showcase the abilities, skills, and mindsets correlated with leadership practice. These individual case studies can serve as role models for students. Diversity in gender and race was a factor in their selection as was the level of contribution each has made to date.
- ◎ *Generalizations about the concept of leadership*: Based on the Taba (1962) Model of Concept Development, the unit is built around eight generalizations about leadership. These generalizations were culled from the theoretical and research base on the construct. Although there are myriad generalizations that can be articulated, the authors crafted these eight with an eye toward their prevalence in the professional literature

DOI:10.4324/9781003233619-2

and their salience for the age of the target population. The generalizations are included in Handout 1.1: Generalizations About Leadership, which is found in Lesson 1.

◎ *Ideas and exercises adapted from contemporary leadership literature*: The unit incorporates ideas and activities that have been adapted from a variety of materials and training guides on how to teach leadership skills. These application exercises have been tailored to high-ability students in middle school.

Unit and Lesson Structure

Changing Tomorrow 2 is composed of 11 lessons that address leadership skill development at the middle school level for students in grades 6–8. Goals and outcomes for the unit focus on inspiring leadership behaviors, enhancing skills in communication and collaboration, understanding the breadth and complexity of the concept itself, and strengthening metacognitive development. The unit also includes a pre- and postassessment on the concept of leadership that can serve as the basis for measuring student learning gains and instructional effectiveness.

Appendix A contains the Teachers' Rap Sheets, which consist of completed Biographical Charts for each of the leaders studied. They are not intended for distribution to students as they are akin to answer keys, but they will streamline the teacher's preparation process. An annotated bibliography in Appendix B details the scholarship that underpins unit conceptualization, design, and content selection.

The instructional component of the unit is composed of 11 substantive lessons; most lessons are subdivided into four or five parts, resulting in about 35 hours of teaching time across the whole unit. Four of the lessons are overarching in scope. Lesson 1 focuses on the introduction of the concept of leadership itself and is constructivist in orientation. Lesson 9 has students share their presentations and the product they chose to develop to illustrate the life of an eminent person studied during the unit. Lesson 10 gives a panel of experts the opportunity to dialogue with students about these big ideas and real-world applications. Lesson 11 includes a final synthesis that requires students to integrate information from the individual case studies.

Seven of the lessons feature biographical case studies of famous world figures in different areas of contribution, including the arts, literature, world politics, and scientific innovation and creativity. Each of the figures demonstrates multiple generalizations about leadership, from having vision, to communicating effectively, to motivating others, to initiating important deeds and work, to persevering in the face of adversity. They also all demonstrate well the interplay of inner and outer forces that come together to make leaders effective in a given domain. The leaders show how innovation and creativity on the part of individuals can lead to a lasting contribution to society. In the cases of Robert Ballard (Lesson 2) and Charles Darwin (Lesson 3), we see two scientists grappling with understanding concepts beyond current understanding and rendering them empirically sound. In the cases of Duke Ellington (Lesson 5) and Pablo Picasso (Lesson 6), we see two giants in the artistic world create new forms and media through which to express the human condition. In the cases of Margaret Thatcher (Lesson 4) and Nelson Mandela (Lesson 8), we see two 20th-century leaders of the world reveal how their life histories prepared them for their role in leading governments. Finally, in Emily Dickinson (Lesson 7), we see the gifted introvert whose outward demeanor would suggest nothing of her inward capacities to create new poetic form and meaning *multum in parvo*. Yet taken together, these seven luminaries illustrate well the generalizations of the unit.

Across the seven biographical lessons, there are some common threads. Each lesson begins with the in-class amalgamation of biographical information from the independent research students have conducted as homework. Students are expected to complete a Biographical Chart for each leader studied that requires them to abstract, prioritize, and summarize information on their own. In Part I of the in-class portion of each biographical lesson, students work with the teacher to create a master chart to ensure that there is a common understanding of the important elements of the leader's life. Part II of each of these lessons uses questioning techniques that require students to analyze, evaluate, and synthesize information, linking the leader's biography to the concept of leadership. Part III of most lessons is an application of a task derived from one of the generalizations studied in the unit. Part IV is typically focused on metacognitive awareness, using journal writing or other task demands that encourage self-reflection on the person and ideas studied and how they relate to the students' own leadership potential and development. Each instructional lesson concludes with student handouts.

In addition to the instructional parts, most lessons contain Assessment, Homework, and Extensions sections. Many of the extensions can be substituted for in-class work or homework, but they are primarily designed for independent study for individual students or small clusters of students.

Technology Requirements

The unit relies heavily on student access to the Internet to do the biographical research, and some lessons require that videos from the Internet be shown to the class as a component of an instructional activity. Suggested websites are included as starting points for students to begin their Internet research; however, the teacher can select additional sites for students to use as he or she sees fit. The teacher will also need to reproduce the handouts in the unit for distribution to the students.

Adapting the Unit for Local Needs

Like a three-dimensional jigsaw puzzle, the pieces of this unit on leadership interlock to ensure that the goals and outcomes are well covered. However, in education one size does not fit all classrooms. In order to make adjustments that will best suit local school parameters, the authors recommend that teachers first read all 11 lessons. This will reveal how the parts of each lesson tie together and build upon one another as the unit progresses.

If adjustments are needed, here are some ideas for consideration:

◎ The biographical research can be done as an in-class activity. In most instances, this will add another period to the length of the whole lesson. In districts where home access to computers is limited and public libraries are not easily accessible, this adaptation would still allow the unit to be taught. If done as an in-class activity, the number of elements students have to document should be reduced from five to three.

◎ The task requirements for the completion of the Biographical Charts by students can be stratified. The preferred model is that all students complete all assigned elements in the Biographical Chart. If this is too time-consuming and/or too repetitive, students can take responsibility for different elements in the chart. All students should read or view all of the material assigned for the research, but the time allocated to documenting the knowledge regarding a leader's life story can be reduced with this approach.

◎ The unit is designed for consecutive sequencing in the curriculum, and Parts I and II of each lesson should be delivered back to back. However, in some lessons, there can be spacing between Parts II and III without great loss in instructional continuity.

◎ Journal writing, which is typically found in Part IV of the lessons, can be done as homework. Teachers can preselect the questions they wish students to explore.

Three Clarifications to Facilitate Unit Implementation

The authors offer three clarifications as a kind of "heads up" in implementing this unit:

- ◎ There is a section included on the Teachers' Rap Sheet that is omitted on the student's blank Biographical Chart for each leader studied. The section is called Lasting Impact and Contributions. In the set of questions provided in Part II of each of the biographical lessons, there is a question asking students to identify these for each leader studied. Students were not asked to document this information as part of the homework because the intent is to get them to think on their feet during class to respond to this prompt.

- ◎ The Internet research on the seven leaders studied is the primary basis for homework in the unit. In order to help students budget their time for conducting this research, teachers may want to distribute the full list of leaders studied, the recommended websites, and the due dates for completion of the Biographical Charts at the end of the first class session. This will ensure that students have plenty of time to complete the homework before each new lesson is started.

- ◎ There is intentional overlap on some of the Internet sites to which students are directed; their rereading of biographical material is designed to reinforce it in their memory banks. Although students are not tested on these biographical details, they need to have a fairly comprehensive knowledge of each leader's life story in order to construct responses to the questions pondered in the in-class discussions and in journal entries.

Curriculum Framework:
Goals and Outcomes of
Changing Tomorrow 2

The following are goals and outcomes of *Changing Tomorrow 2*.

1. To provide role models for young people that will inspire leadership by example as an encouragement to seek and fulfill leadership roles and responsibilities for themselves. Students will be able to:
    o conduct biographical research on leaders using the Internet,
    o identify and evaluate the characteristics and skills of various leaders, and
    o synthesize the factors that contribute to effective leadership, including the talent development process.

2. To develop skills in communication and collaboration to deepen student understanding of the complex demands and challenges of leadership. Students will be able to:
    o develop listening skills that promote their understanding of other perspectives,
    o articulate their ideas in written and oral form, and
    o work individually and in multiple group settings to carry out an agenda or execute a sophisticated task demand requiring more than one person's effort.

3. To understand the construct of leadership as it manifests within and across various fields of human endeavor. Students will be able to:
    o construct a definition of leadership,
    o elaborate on team-building and conflict resolution skills as dimensions of effective leadership, and
    o apply leadership knowledge and/or skills to real-world problem resolution.

4. To develop metacognitive skills that will strengthen leadership capacity-building. Students will be able to:
    o articulate the skill sets and habits of mind of past and present leaders,

DOI:10.4324/9781003233619-3

o create products that reflect an understanding of leadership expectations and/or apply and assess selected leadership skills in carrying out multilayered task demands, and

o reflect on their own leadership strengths and weaknesses through the creation of a personal profile.

Alignment
of the *Changing Tomorrow* Series With National Standards

In any new curriculum endeavor for gifted learners, it is crucial to show how it responds to the national view of curriculum standards in relevant areas. The following alignment framework shows how the *Changing Tomorrow* units respond to the 2010 NAGC Pre-K–Grade 12 Gifted Education Programming Standards, 21st-century skills (Partnership for 21st Century Skills, 2011), and the Common Core State Standards for English Language Arts (National Governors Association Center for Best Practices & Council of Chief State School Officers, 2010).

Alignment to the NAGC Pre-K–Grade 12 Gifted Education Programming Standards in Curriculum and Assessment

The *Changing Tomorrow* units align to the NAGC Pre-K–Grade 12 Gifted Education Programming Standards in the following ways:

◎ *Scope and sequence development*: The *Changing Tomorrow* units offer a set of interrelated emphases/activities for use across grades 4–12, with a common format and within a key concept on leadership with interrelated generalizations.

◎ *Use of differentiation strategies*: The authors used the central differentiation strategies emphasized in the standards, including critical and creative thinking, problem solving, inquiry, research, and concept development.

◎ *Use of acceleration/advancement techniques, including performance pre- and postassessments, formative assessment, and portfolios*: The authors used all of these strategies as well as advanced research skills to ensure a high level of challenge for gifted and advanced students.

◎ *Adaptation or replacement of the core curriculum*: The project extends the Common Core State Standards by ensuring that gifted learners master them and then go beyond them in key ways. Some standards

DOI:10.4324/9781003233619-4

are mastered earlier (e.g., reading and language skills), while others are practiced at higher levels of skill and concept in these leadership units.

◎ *Use of culturally sensitive curriculum approaches leading to cultural competency*: The authors have employed international and American multicultural leaders to ensure that students have an appreciation for the contributions of different cultures to our world today.

◎ *Use of research-based materials*: The authors have included models and techniques found to be highly effective with gifted learners in enhancing critical thinking, text analysis, and persuasive writing. They have also used the questioning techniques found in Junior Great Books and the William and Mary language arts units, both research-based language arts programs used nationally with gifted learners.

◎ *Use of information technologies*: The authors have used biographical research as a central tool for learning in an online environment. They also suggest the use of visual media, computer technology, and multimedia in executing the learning activities developed.

◎ *Use of metacognitive strategies*: The authors have included activities where students use reflection, planning, monitoring, and assessing skills. Each activity includes a journal entry that presses students to reflect on their understanding of leadership.

◎ *Use of community resources*: The units include opportunities for students to learn from a panel of experts or to interview a person central to understanding some aspect of leadership.

◎ *Career development*: Biography is the central reading tool used by the authors for students to learn about an eminent person who has demonstrated leadership skills in a given domain.

◎ *Talent development in areas of aptitude and interest in various domains (cognitive, affective, aesthetic)*: The units present people who have succeeded in various domains of human endeavor. Activities provide multiple opportunities for students to explore domain-specific interests, such as writing, viewing, and oral expression, thus exercising multiple levels of skills in cognitive, affective, and aesthetic areas.

Alignment to 21st-Century Skills

The *Changing Tomorrow* units also include a major emphasis on key 21st-century skills in overall orientation, as well as key activities and assessments employed. Several of these skill sets overlap with the differentiation emphases discussed above in relation to the gifted education standards. The skills receiving major emphasis include:

- ◎ *Collaboration*: Students are encouraged to work in dyads and small groups of four to carry out the research activities, to discuss readings, and to organize information on biographical material.
- ◎ *Communication*: Students are encouraged to develop communication skills in written, oral, visual, and technological modes in a balanced format within each unit of study.
- ◎ *Critical thinking*: Students are provided with models of critical thought that are incorporated into classroom activities, questions, and assignments.
- ◎ *Creative thinking*: Students are provided with models of creative thinking that develop skills that support innovative thinking and problem solving.
- ◎ *Problem solving*: Students are engaged in real-world problem solving in each unit of study and learn the processes involved in such work.
- ◎ *Technology literacy*: Students use technology in multiple forms and formats to create generative products.
- ◎ *Information media literacy*: Students use multimedia to express ideas and project learning.
- ◎ *Cross-cultural skills*: Students read and discuss works and events representing the perspectives of different cultures. They have opportunities to analyze different perspectives on issues.
- ◎ *Social skills*: Students work in small groups and develop the tools of collaboration, communication, and working effectively with others on a common set of tasks.

Alignment to the Common Core State Standards for English Language Arts

In addition to the 21st-century skills listed above, there are other points of integration with important curriculum standards such as the Common Core State Standards (CCSS) for English Language Arts. The units draw deeply on nonfiction literature, predominantly biography, as a basis for biographical study. The units require students to cite textual evidence to support their ideas, to integrate information from multiple sources, and to develop and justify their claims made during in classroom discussion. There is also time dedicated to reflective writing, which helps students develop self-awareness, critical thinking, and intellectual curiosity. Because the standards call for a major emphasis on developing argument, the *Changing Tomorrow* units require gifted and advanced students to analyze data, claims, and warrants in the material they read and to develop arguments on specific issues of leadership based on multiple data sources. As such, the unit is well aligned with the new CCSS.

Part II

Pre- and Postassessments and Rubric

DOI:10.4324/9781003233619-5

Instructions
for the Assessments

One way to help teachers measure both student learning gains and instructional effectiveness is to use a pre- and postassessment tool. In *Changing Tomorrow 2*, this assessment is based on the students' breadth of understanding of the elements of the concept of leadership, using a concept mapping technique. The same testing prompt is used in both the pre- and posttesting process.

Teachers should administer the preassessment before students begin the unit. This may be done on the day before or first day of implementation. Similarly, the postassessment should be administered when the unit has concluded. It can be administered on either the last day of implementation or closely following the last day. The suggested time frame for completing the assessment is 15 minutes.

A rubric is provided to use in scoring the instrument. Teachers should use the preassessment as a basis for judging how much students already know about leadership. The postassessment should be used to judge conceptual growth in understanding leadership.

In addition to sharing the results of the changes in learning with the students themselves, the teacher may want to aggregate the gain scores across all students. If the unit is taught over multiple years to different groups of students, the teacher will have a basis for assessing any improvements in instructional effectiveness over time. The scoring of the instrument should also lead to insights about what students absorbed or failed to absorb as a result of their experience in the classroom.

DOI:10.4324/9781003233619-6

Preassessment
on the Concept of Leadership

(15 minutes)

Create a concept map to illustrate your understanding of the concept of leadership as we begin this unit of study. Draw a circle and put the word leadership in the center. Then, draw connections to that circle that describe how you understand the concept. Make as many connections as you can and label them. Then, describe the nature of the connections you have drawn.

Are there other things you know about leadership that you have not put in the concept map? Please add them below.

DOI:10.4324/9781003233619-7

Changing Tomorrow 2, Grades 6–8 © Taylor & Francis Inc.

Postassessment
on the Concept of Leadership

(15 minutes)

Create a concept map to illustrate your understanding of the concept of leadership as we end this unit of study. Draw a circle and put the word leadership in the center. Then, draw connections to that circle that describe how you understand the concept. Make as many connections as you can and label them. Then, describe the nature of the connections you have drawn.

Are there other things you know about leadership that you have not put in the concept map? Please add them below.

DOI:10.4324/9781003233619-8

Rubric for Scoring
the Pre- and Postassessments
on the Concept of Leadership

Please score each student paper according to the following dimensions of the activity. The scale goes from a 4 (*high*) to a 1 (*low*).

1. Students make appropriate *numbers* of connections to the concept.			
1 *(1–2 given)*	**2** *(3–4 given)*	**3** *(5–7 given)*	**4** *(at least 8 examples given)*

2. Students make different *types* of connections to the concept.			
1 *(only one type of connection is provided)*	**2** *(two types are provided)*	**3** *(three types are provided)*	**4** *(four or more types are provided)*

3. Students provide an apt description of the aspect of the concept delineated or the relationship of the concept to its connection.			
1 *(only one apt description is provided)*	**2** *(two apt descriptions are provided)*	**3** *(three apt descriptions are provided)*	**4** *(four or more apt descriptions are provided)*

4. For additional ideas contributed about leadership, students should receive one point each, raising their score totals in uneven ways.

Add all point totals from the above items together to arrive at a student score. The top score would be 12+, depending on the fourth item on the rubric.

DOI:10.4324/9781003233619-9

Changing Tomorrow 2, Grades 6–8 © Taylor & Francis Inc.

Part III
Lessons

DOI:10.4324/9781003233619-10

Lesson 1
Introduction to the Concept of Leadership

Instructional Purpose
- To introduce the concept of leadership
- To share unit generalizations

Materials Needed
- Chart paper
- Markers
- Handout 1.1: Generalizations About Leadership
- Handout 1.2: Specifications for Student-Directed Project on Leadership
- Handout 1.3: Rubric for Student-Directed Project on Leadership

Activities and Instructional Strategies

This lesson is constructivist in orientation, so teachers need to follow the script offered below when teaching it. Students need to come up with their own ideas about leadership as the unit begins.

Part I (50 minutes)

1. Place students in groups of 3–5 to complete the following activities:
   - Ask students to name as many people as they can who are leaders in American society. They should try to list at least 25.
   - Have students make their list on chart paper and share the examples by group. As each group adds new examples, the teacher should generate a master chart of names.
   - Groups should then categorize the domains in which their lists of leaders have contributed.
   - Ask students to share their categories by groups. Create a master list of the domains of leadership generated. Ask students why some categories have several leaders but others have so few.
   - Ask: What are some examples of leadership qualities needed to perform in these domains? Discuss a few and write them on the master list.

DOI:10.4324/9781003233619-11

o Have students list nonexamples (people who are not exemplary of leadership qualities). Once they are finished brainstorming, have the groups share their examples. Make a master list.

o Ask: What do these people have in common? What qualities do you think keep them from being leaders? Discuss as a whole class.

o Instruct the groups to generate 2–3 generalizations about leadership. Ask: How do these generalizations apply to all of your examples and none of your nonexamples?

o Have students contribute their generalizations to the master chart. Do they all fit the people generated as examples?

Part II (1 period)

1. In their groups, ask students to review their list of generalizations, as well as the unit generalizations (Handout 1.1: Generalizations About Leadership), and do the following:

   o Indicate which ones from their list are similar to the ones found in the unit.

   o Decide which unit generalizations apply to examples of people the group generated.

   o Determine which generalizations do not fit the work done thus far.

   o Tell students that both sets of generalizations will guide their development of understanding the concept of leadership better as they explore it through reading the biographies of great Americans, both contemporary and from the past.

2. Now ask students to generate a list of leadership qualities that they consider important, based on their work. Have each group share its list and create a master list for reference during the unit.

3. Ask students to choose one quality of leadership and write a one-paragraph argument supporting its importance for all leaders to possess. (Allow 15 minutes for the writing activity.)

4. Ask students to share 3–5 examples orally. Have students begin a portfolio of their writing for use during the unit and include this piece as their first entry.

Part III (50 minutes)

1. Pass out Handout 1.2: Specifications for Student-Directed Project on Leadership to students and discuss the parameters for their independent study project on leadership. Answer questions as they arise. Some of the extension activities generated for each of the seven leaders studied in this

book may be considered for this project, based on student interest and teacher judgment.

2. Students should use the following guiding questions as they prepare their presentation:
   o What early life experiences impacted the development of talent in this person?
   o What people played an important role in the talent development process? In what ways?
   o What interests and passions were ignited in this person to provoke extraordinary accomplishment in adulthood? How and when did this occur?
   o What were the major accomplishments? How was the person rewarded for the work?
   o What legacy has this person left on his or her field?
   o What qualities of leadership did this person exhibit?
   o Why have you chosen the product you have developed as the appropriate venue for representing this person's talent?

3. Share Handout 1.3: Rubric for Student-Directed Project on Leadership with students so they understand the criteria on which their project will be assessed.

4. Remind students to make their choice of project options no later than the following week so they may begin their work.

Assessment

Teachers should use the constructed work of students as the basis for judging their initial understanding of the concept of leadership.

Homework

Students should read the material at the following websites on Robert Ballard, the first leader studied in the unit.
   ◎ Wikipedia (http://en.wikipedia.org/wiki/Robert_Ballard)
   ◎ Encyclopedia.com (http://www.encyclopedia.com/topic/Robert_Duane _Ballard.aspx)
   ◎ Academy of Achievement (http://achievement.org/autodoc/page/bal0 bio-1)
   ◎ Premiere Motivational Speakers Bureau (http://premierespeakers.com/ robert_ballard/bio)
   ◎ National Geographic (http://www.nationalgeographic.com/explorers/ bios/robert-ballard/)

They should be given a copy of Handout 2.1: Biographical Chart: Robert Ballard, found in the next lesson, to help guide their reading and to use for taking notes. Students should be instructed to fill out each element in the Biographical Chart with four or five pieces of information about Dr. Ballard drawn from the readings. Students must read all five of the biographical entries and select important facts to include on their charts.

Handout 1.1

Generalizations About Leadership

⊚ Leadership requires vision—the ability to see beyond what is to what might be by bridging the present and the future.

⊚ Leadership requires the ability to communicate effectively with multiple individuals and groups regarding new ideas and plans for implementation.

⊚ Leadership is based in action and often requires risk taking.

⊚ Leadership requires the ability to influence and motivate others through words and actions.

⊚ Leadership requires perseverance in the face of challenges and hardships.

⊚ Leadership creates legacies that are best understood after the passage of time.

⊚ Leadership is highly dependent on the interplay of intellectual abilities, specific aptitudes and skills, and personality factors.

⊚ Leadership has shared and unique features across fields.

Specifications for Student–Directed Project on Leadership

Directions: You will select a product option from the list below by next week in order to conduct an independent study on one leader. The presentation and product are due in 6 weeks. Some time may be given to help you prepare in class. However, all readings for this project should be done outside of class. You will be assessed on your presentation and your product (see Handout 1.3: Rubric for Student-Directed Project on Leadership).

◎ *Option #1*: Read a complete biography of a person of your choice not covered in this unit and prepare a PowerPoint presentation about this person, highlighting the talent development process in his or her life. Some options include:

- Barbara McClintock, scientist
- César Chávez, social reformer
- Mao Tse-tung, political leader
- August Wilson, playwright
- Diego Rivera, artist
- Henry Ford, inventor and entrepreneur
- Oprah Winfrey, entertainer
- Charles Dickens, writer
- Gustav Mahler, musician
- Plato or Aristotle, philosophers

◎ *Option #2*: Take a generalization about leadership and read multiple (at least three) short biographies of people not studied in this unit to show different ways that aspect of leadership was exemplified either within or across fields. Create a product to display your findings (e.g., a poster, a PowerPoint presentation, a film or other type of multimedia project, a written piece).

◎ *Option #3*: Create a written speech that models key dimensions of leadership seen in either Margaret Thatcher or Nelson Mandela.

◎ *Option #4*: Prepare a student-generated product of choice approved by the teacher.

Name: _____ Date: _____

Rubric for Student-Directed Project on Leadership

Please score each student project according to the following dimensions of the activity. The scale goes from a 4 (*high*) to a 1 (*low*).

Criteria	4	3	2	1
Adherence to guidelines	The project meets all guidelines.	The project meets most guidelines.	The project meets few guidelines.	The project meets no guidelines.
Organization	The project is very well organized and delineated by sections.	The project is well organized and delineated by sections.	The project is somewhat organized but lacks clear delineation of required features.	The project lacks meaningful organization.
Content	The project demonstrates very strong content knowledge of the material.	The project demonstrates strong content knowledge of the material.	The project demonstrates limited content knowledge of the material.	The project demonstrates lack of content knowledge.
Creativity	The project demonstrates very strong evidence of originality and elaboration.	The project demonstrates strong evidence of originality and elaboration.	The project shows limited use of originality and elaboration of ideas.	The project lacks originality and elaboration of ideas.
Use of visual media	The project uses visual media very effectively to portray project ideas.	The project uses visual media effectively to portray project ideas.	The project uses visual media ineffectively to portray project ideas.	The project does not employ visual media for portraying ideas.

Lesson 2
Robert Ballard

All kids dream a marvelous image of what they want to do. But then society tells them they can't do it. I didn't listen. I wanted to live my dream.

—Robert Ballard

Instructional Purpose

◎ To practice using the Internet to do biographical research
◎ To map the biographical data against key leadership factors
◎ To practice using listening and reasoning skills in constructing written arguments
◎ To advocate a position with regard to a real-world problem

Materials Needed

◎ Handout 2.1: Biographical Chart: Robert Ballard
◎ Handout 2.2: Study Guide for Robert Ballard's Speech
◎ Answer Key for Handout 2.2: Study Guide for Robert Ballard's Speech
◎ Teachers' Rap Sheet for Robert Ballard (see Appendix A)

Activities and Instructional Strategies

Part I (2 periods)

1. Check that the Biographical Chart for Robert Ballard has been completed.
2. Have the whole class complete a master Biographical Chart by using a white board or overhead projector to compile the information gathered by students. The teacher should start by asking: What did you discover about Dr. Ballard's early family background and created family structure? What did you discover about his education? Follow this format until the master chart has been completed enough to ensure that the students have a fairly in-depth profile of the individual. The teacher may choose to annotate or extend the information in the Biographical Chart by drawing on the data provided in the Teachers' Rap Sheet found in Appendix A. Students should embellish their own charts as the class session unfolds.
3. Because this is the first lesson involving student research using Internet sites, the teacher may prefer to use in-class time to have students conduct the biographical research. If this is done as an in-class activity, additional time should be allocated to carry out this part of the lesson before commencing with the compilation of information on the master chart. In

DOI:10.4324/9781003233619-12

31

addition, the teacher may reduce the number of data points that students collect for each element from four or five to three to save time in documentation. Refer to the Homework section of the previous lesson to find the website references to give to the students.

4. An additional option for compressing time if doing the research as an in-class activity is to stratify the elements assigned to individual students for data collection. Students would still have to read of all the material, but they would only need to document the data points for the specific elements assigned to them.

Part II (1 period)

1. The teacher will engage students in a large-group discussion using the following questions:
   o In what ways is Robert Ballard a leader?
   o To what extent did time, place, and circumstances impact his ability to become a leader?
   o How would you describe the vision that Robert Ballard has brought to the field of oceanography? In what ways are exploration of space and the oceans alike? In what ways are they different?
   o What personal characteristics contributed to Robert Ballard's success as an explorer and scientist?
   o What evidence is there of both initiative and risk taking in Dr. Ballard's profile?
   o What do you see as Dr. Ballard's lasting impact and contributions in the field of oceanography based on what you know at this time? What specific innovations did he pioneer in his area of expertise?
   o Robert Ballard said: "Science is a 'we' not an 'I.' I didn't do anything. We did a lot of things. But in our system in America we have this star-based system. Star athletes, star news people, star politicians. And stars are 'I.' And the academic world is really, honestly a 'we.'" What does he mean by this statement? Do you agree that athletics, broadcasting, and politics are not team-driven enterprises? Can you name any "stars" in science? What about art? Is art tilted toward the individual or the group? In what ways?

Part III (1+ period)

1. Distribute Handout 2.2: Study Guide for Robert Ballard's Speech for students to review prior to watching the 18-minute video clip on TED.com of Dr. Ballard's speech on "Exploring the Oceans" (http://www.ted.com/talks/robert_ballard_on_exploring_the_oceans.html). Broadcast the

video of the speech to the whole class or direct students to computers to allow them to watch the speech and give them an additional 10 minutes to complete Handout 2.2.

2. Break the class into teams of 3–5 students and have them review their answers to Handout 2.2. (Answers to the questions are included for the teacher at the end of the lesson. These answers are intended to help the teacher guide the small-group discussions of the student responses, not to grade their answers. The answer key should *not* be distributed to students.) Allow only 10 minutes to complete this process, as its purpose is to ensure that students have grasped the major ideas in the speech as well as some of the important facts presented. Monitor the groups to ensure that they are moving rapidly through this review and clarification exercise. Ask the groups if there are any questions and briefly clarify information as needed.

3. Keep the students in groups and tell them that since the speech was given in 2008, funding for both space and oceanic exploration by the federal government was slightly increased each year until 2011, but the National Aeronautics and Space Administration (NASA) has received about $18 billion each year, and the National Oceanic and Atmospheric Administration (NOAA) has received about $5 billion. Explain that the dollar amount for research and development is only a portion of the funding that is given to each of these agencies, which is why the reference in Dr. Ballard's speech is not consistent with this ratio. As a caveat, mention the recent controversy around the dismantling of the successor to the shuttle program at NASA, an initiative called Constellation, and the change in federal space exploration policy to privatize future flights to the moon.

4. Ask each group to advocate for increased federal funding for research and development for either NOAA or NASA by developing at least three arguments to support the agency's position. As the groups report their results to the rest of the class, the teacher should compile a nonduplicative listing of the arguments presented on the board. This listing should be used to help groups create master letters incorporating all of the reasons in support of additional funding for each federal program. Have the class help edit these master letters into a formal letter to the President of the United States. If two letters have been drafted (one for each federal program), ask the class which of the letters they, as a whole group, would like to send on to the White House. If time does not allow for this to be done as an in-class activity, ask for volunteers to serve on a committee to polish the final letter so that it is clear, cogent, and articulate. During the

next class period or at some reasonable interval, have the final version of the letter read and approved by the whole class prior to sending it.

Part IV (1 period)

1. The teacher will allow 10–15 minutes for students to complete their journals using some or all of the following questions as prompts. These questions may be put on the board or can be made into a handout that is inserted into the students' journals.
   - What did you learn from the biographical study of Robert Ballard that is useful or interesting in your understanding of leadership?
   - What invention or discovery made by Dr. Ballard and his colleagues do you think is the most important and why?
   - In what ways is Robert Ballard a role model for you and other young leaders?
   - What did you learn about Internet research by going through this process?
   - What did you learn about the role of advocacy in solving real-world problems? In what ways did Dr. Ballard model effective advocacy for his position on oceanic exploration?

2. Ask a few students to share their responses with the whole class.
3. As an alternative to an in-class activity, the teacher may assign this as part of the homework.

Assessment

The teacher should check to see that each student has completed the Biographical Chart on Robert Ballard, Handout 2.2, and the journal entry and include it in the student's portfolio. In addition, a copy of the class letter to the President should be inserted into the student's portfolio.

Homework

Students are assigned responsibility for completing Handout 3.1: Biographical Chart: Charles Darwin in preparation for the next class period. The sites that students may be directed to for conducting this research are as follows:
- Wikipedia (http://en.wikipedia.org/wiki/Charles_Darwin)
- Darwin Online (http://darwin-online.org.uk)
- AboutDarwin.com (http://www.aboutdarwin.com)
- Questia (http://www.questia.com/library/science-and-technology/scientists-and-inventors/charles-darwin)

Extensions

The following ideas are offered as substitutions for parts of the above lesson or as extensions for this lesson focusing on Robert Ballard.

◎ Have students critique the speech by Dr. Ballard in terms of its effectiveness in persuading people to support his point of view. This critique should focus on identifying the purpose of the speech and the techniques used to persuade his audience (e.g., build trust in your audience or team; show confidence, conviction, and enthusiasm; stay on message, and be clear and precise; use graphic aids, such as pictures, charts, and graphs, to illustrate and clarify important points; use stories, metaphors, and symbols to entertain and inspire; and use humor in an appropriate way). In addition, have students comment on the speech's effectiveness in influencing them, and have them identify the next steps that can be taken to address the problem cited in the speech.

◎ Have students explore the concept of vision by writing a vision statement for the colonization of the sea by the U.S. government or private entrepreneurs. They may do this as individuals or in small groups. Have them create a motto and a logo for implementing this enterprise.

◎ For independent work, encourage students to read one of the early books written by Dr. Ballard himself (for advanced readers) or the middle-school-level biography of him by Lisa Yount entitled *Robert Ballard: Explorer and Undersea Archaeologist*. Instead of having students write a traditional book report, ask them to identify examples of how Dr. Ballard exhibited at least three of the generalizations on leadership addressed in this unit.

◎ Have students watch the *60 Minutes* interview with Dr. Ballard (http://www.cbsnews.com/2100-18560_162-6568485.html) and develop a profile of Dr. Ballard's leadership skills as illustrated in his behavior and remarks.

◎ Have students go to the live web feed of the *Nautilus* (http://www.nautiluslive.org) and explore the features available on it. Have them suggest an idea for another live scientific webcast and design a home page for their idea.

Handout 2.1

Biographical Chart: Robert Ballard

Full Name: _____

Lifespan: _____

Early Family Background and Created Family Structure

_____

_____

_____

Personality Characteristics and Areas of Aptitude, Talent, and Interest

_____

_____

_____

Major Career/Professional Events and Accomplishments

_____

_____

_____

Personal Life Themes/Beliefs

_____

_____

_____

Selected Quotations

_____

_____

_____

Awards and Recognition

_____

_____

_____

_____

Handout 2.2

Study Guide for Robert Ballard's Speech

1. What is the opening question around which Dr. Ballard organizes his remarks?

2. What is the relationship of one year of NASA funding to one year of NOAA funding for research and exploration?

3. What percent of the planet is under water?

4. How were many discoveries made in this field of science?

5. What percent of the U.S. lies beneath water?

6. What is the greatest mountain range on Earth, and what percent of the Earth's surface does it cover?

7. In what year did the first human beings enter the Rift Valley?

8. What are some of the discoveries that have been made in oceanic exploration under Dr. Ballard's leadership?

9. By what grade level do students usually decide whether or not they want to become scientists or engineers?

10. What is the closing question that Dr. Ballard asks his audience to think about?

Answer Key for Handout 2.2:

Study Guide for Robert Ballard's Speech

(Not for distribution to students)

1. What is the opening question around which Dr. Ballard organizes his remarks?

   The opening question is: Why are we ignoring the oceans in our scientific exploration programs?

2. What is the relationship of one year of NASA funding to one year of NOAA funding for research and exploration?

   One year of NASA funding is equal to 1,600 years of NOAA funding for research and exploration.

3. What percent of the planet is under water?

   Seventy-two percent of the planet is under water.

4. How were many discoveries made in this field of science?

   Many of the discoveries in this field of science were actually made by accident.

5. What percent of the U.S. lies beneath water?

   Fifty percent of the U.S. lies beneath the water.

6. What is the greatest mountain range on Earth, and what percent of the Earth's surface does it cover?

   The Mid-Ocean Ridge is the greatest mountain range and covers approximately 23% of the Earth's surface.

7. In what year did the first human beings enter the Rift Valley?

   The first human beings entered the great Rift Valley in 1973, and Dr. Ballard was one of them.

8. What are some of the discoveries that have been made in oceanic exploration under Dr. Ballard's leadership?

   Dr. Ballard found that there were hot springs with heavy metal deposits, which explained the missing heat in the ridge; discovered a profusion of life heretofore unknown using chemosynthesis rather than photosynthesis; found a "lost city" of limestone formations with pH levels of 11; and located ships and realized how the ocean has preserved artifacts rivaling the great history museums of the world.

9. By what grade level do students usually decide whether or not they want to become scientists or engineers?
   Students will decide by eighth grade.

10. What is the closing question that Dr. Ballard asks his audience to think about?
    The closing question is: Why don't we have programs to colonize the sea?

Lesson 3
Charles Darwin

As many more individuals of each species are born than can possibly survive; and as, consequently, there is a frequently recurring struggle for existence, it follows that any being, if it vary however slightly in any manner profitable to itself, under the complex and sometimes varying conditions of life, will have a better chance of surviving, and thus be naturally selected.

—Charles Darwin

Instructional Purpose

- ◎ To practice using the Internet to do biographical research
- ◎ To map biographical data against key leadership factors
- ◎ To develop oral and written communication skills

Materials

- ◎ Handout 3.1: Biographical Chart: Charles Darwin
- ◎ Teachers' Rap Sheet on Charles Darwin (see Appendix A)

Activities and Instructional Strategies

Part I (1 period)

1. Have students break into groups to discuss their findings about Charles Darwin, based on the information students found from completing their prior homework assignment research.
2. Have the whole class complete a master Biographical Chart on Charles Darwin, based on the information students found from completing their prior homework assignment research. This should be done using a white board or overhead projector, as was done in Lesson 2. Again, as in Lesson 2, the teacher should use questioning techniques to gather the data needed to complete a master chart. The teacher may choose to annotate the information collected by drawing on the Teachers' Rap Sheet for Mr. Darwin if students have failed to grasp and/or record important pieces of biographical information.
3. Engage students in a large-group discussion using the following questions:
   - ○ Darwin was an amateur scientist when he boarded the HMS *Beagle*. What accounted for his conversion to a serious scientist?
   - ○ Being a leader in a field often means seeing beyond the present to a future not yet imagined. How did Darwin's theory impact our thinking about the world?

DOI:10.4324/9781003233619-13

o In 1988, the Human Genome Project began, whereby human DNA could be mapped to determine genetic anomalies. How does this project depend on Darwin's theory of evolution?

o Darwin spent the last 20 years of his life suffering from serious illnesses that were never satisfactorily diagnosed (he was often told his illnesses were from overwork). Based on your analysis of his biography and work, what characteristics did Darwin possess that might have contributed to his illnesses?

o Darwin was also a family man who enjoyed spending time with his large family. What role did he play in shaping their interests and subsequent careers?

o Alfred Russel Wallace proposed evolutionary theory at the same time Darwin was writing his paper on the origin of species. What explains the similarity of findings of the two men? How did scientists of the time view the discovery?

Part II (2–4 periods)

1. Darwin's work has been perceived by many to be the most important discovery of all time in the world of science. Others reject the theory of evolution in favor of creationism, a theory that argues for intelligent design by a greater power. Ask students to form debate teams to argue the proposition: Evolution should be considered the most significant scientific discovery. Each debate team should consist of five students who prepare and carry out their side of the debate, based on the following roles:
   o Student #1: Affirmative (5 minutes)
   o Student #2: Negative (5 minutes)
   o Student #3: Affirmative rebuttal (3 minutes)
   o Student #4: Negative rebuttal (3 minutes)
   o Student #5: Critique of the argument (5 minutes)

2. Preparation for the debate may take one period, and the debates may take two periods, depending on the size of the class. The teacher should comment on each group's presentation with respect to the following criteria:
   o organization,
   o clarity of the argument,
   o strength of the argument based on data,
   o ability to synthesize data, and
   o ability to evaluate evidence.

Part III (1 period)

1. The teacher will share the following with students: Darwin exemplified a famous scientist whose work has endured and continues to influence our thinking today. Yet, scientists are different from other leaders in that it is their ideas and related discoveries that matter the most with respect to their role in human affairs.
2. Have students write a journal entry that comments on how a scientist is a leader. Students should use the generalizations on leadership as a basis for their commentary, applying at least two of them to their argument (see Handout 1.1 from Lesson 1).
3. After students have finished their journal writing, have 3–5 students share their thoughts on the prompt. Discuss as appropriate and as time permits.

Assessment

The teacher should use the debate criteria to judge the effectiveness of each team's presentation. The teacher should also review the journal entries to ensure that students are making the right connections from the data on Charles Darwin to the generalizations about leadership.

Homework

Students are assigned responsibility for completing Handout 4.1: Biographical Chart: Margaret Thatcher in preparation for the next class period. The three sites that students should be directed to for conducting this research are as follows:
 ◎ Wikipedia (http://en.wikipedia.org/wiki/Margaret_Thatcher)
 ◎ Biography.com (http://www.biography.com/people/margaret-thatcher-9504796)
 ◎ Margaret Thatcher Foundation (http://www.margaretthatcher.org)

The teacher should remind students to read the material on all there of the websites even though they only have to document four or five examples of each element on the chart. As an option, the teacher may stratify the documentation requirements by assigning only selected elements to each student so that the chart can be completed in Part I of the next lesson by the class as a whole.

Extensions

The following ideas are offered as substitutions for parts of the above lesson or as extensions for this lesson focusing on Charles Darwin.
 ◎ Have students read three papers by Darwin and share the major findings from the papers in a three-page report.

◎ Many biographies have been written about Charles Darwin. Allow students to select one and read it for evidence of his contributions to science. Students should develop a timeline of Darwin's accomplishments that begins with his voyage on the HMS *Beagle* and ends with his death.

◎ Darwin came from an illustrious family and produced one as well. Have students read Sir Francis Galton's work on hereditary genius and link Darwin's family as an example of his theory. (Sir Francis Galton was Darwin's cousin.)

Handout 3.1

Biographical Chart: Charles Darwin

Full Name: _____

Lifespan: _____

Early Family Background and Created Family Structure

_____

_____

_____

Personality Characteristics and Areas of Aptitude, Talent, and Interest

_____

_____

_____

Major Career/Professional Events and Accomplishments

_____

_____

_____

Personal Life Themes/Beliefs

_____

_____

_____

Selected Quotations

_____

_____

_____

Awards and Recognition

_____

_____

_____

_____

Lesson 4
Margaret Thatcher

If you just set out to be liked, you would be prepared to compromise on anything at any time, and you would achieve nothing.

—Margaret Thatcher

Instructional Purpose

- To practice using the Internet to conduct biographical research
- To map biographical data against key leadership factors
- To analyze one's own leadership abilities

Materials

- Handout 4.1: Biographical Chart: Margaret Thatcher
- Handout 4.2: Self-Assessment of Leadership
- Handout 4.3: Self-Assessment: Success Query
- Teachers' Rap Sheet on Margaret Thatcher (see Appendix A)

Activities and Instructional Strategies

Part I (1–2 periods)

1. The teacher will break the students into triads or groups of four and have each group complete a master Biographical Chart by sharing the information collected on Margaret Thatcher for homework. Upon completion of the full chart by each group, the teacher will reconvene the whole class to fill in any blanks or to correct any misunderstandings regarding the biographical details of Ms. Thatcher's life. To start this process, the teacher will ask one of the small groups to share the information it compiled for the first two sections of the chart.
2. The teacher will then ask if anyone else in the class has information to add to these two sections of the chart.
3. Before going onto the next sections of the chart, ask: Do you have any questions about the information in these two sections of the chart? The teacher should use a parallel process and set of questions for the remaining sections on the chart. As in prior lessons, the teacher may choose to annotate or expand upon the information compiled by students by drawing on the Teachers' Rap Sheet for Ms. Thatcher.

DOI:10.4324/9781003233619-14

Part II (1–2 periods)

1. The teacher should ask the following questions as a prelude to the in-class writing assignment:
   o What was Margaret Thatcher's style of leadership? Why do you think she adopted it?
   o The Soviets called her the "Iron Lady." What does that mean in the context of her leadership in England?
   o What were Thatcher's ways of persuading others to do as she wanted?
   o What were her greatest accomplishments as a politician?
   o How did Margaret Thatcher's early upbringing influence her?
   o The role of vision is critical in sustaining leadership. What aspects of the time period in which she led did Margaret Thatcher understand and act on?

2. Ask students to complete the following persuasive writing activity: Many critics of Margaret Thatcher saw her impact on Britain as negative, whereas her supporters saw her role as essentially positive. What is your view? Support your claim with evidence from your research. Students should spend 30 minutes responding to it.

Part III (1 period)

1. Have students complete Handout 4.2: Self-Assessment of Leadership.
2. Discuss student responses regarding their personalities and perceived leadership skills.
3. The teacher should begin the discussion by asking:
   o Who are your role models for leadership? Why?
   o How does your understanding of your personality and leadership skills affect your thinking about a career?
   o What would be your ratings for Margaret Thatcher on these scales? What top leadership skills did she display? Support your point of view.
   o What process will you use to engage in decision making about career choices?

Assessment

The teacher should check to see that each student has completed the Biographical Chart on Margaret Thatcher. The teacher should use the persuasive writing piece at the end of Part II to judge individual student progress in this lesson. The teacher should insert the completed Handout 4.2 into each student's portfolio.

Homework

Ask students to complete Handout 4.3: Self-Assessment: Success Query as homework.

Extensions

◎ Have students read one of the complete biographies on Margaret Thatcher. Students can select a product of their choice to summarize what they learned.

◎ Ask students to critique the film, *The Iron Lady*. Students should decide whether they think the film is fair in its portrayal of the life of Margaret Thatcher and explain why or why not.

◎ Have students read three speeches by Margaret Thatcher and analyze her ideas and style of writing. Students should summarize their findings in a poster.

Handout 4.1

Biographical Chart: Margaret Thatcher

Full Name: _____

Lifespan: _____

Early Family Background and Created Family Structure

_____

_____

_____

Personality Characteristics and Areas of Aptitude, Talent, and Interest

_____

_____

_____

Major Career/Professional Events and Accomplishments

_____

_____

_____

Personal Life Themes/Beliefs

_____

_____

_____

Selected Quotations

_____

_____

_____

Awards and Recognition

_____

_____

_____

_____

Name: _____ Date: _____

Self–Assessment of Leadership

Part I

Directions: Using the following rating skill, place an X in the column that most accurately describes your development/mastery level for each of the skills specified.

NA = Not Applicable at This Time	1 = Minimal
2 = Developing (In Progress) 3 = Proficient	4 = Excellent

Categories and Skill Sets	Rating				
	NA	1	2	3	4
Visioning Skills					
• Can relate to and describe the big picture					
• Can conceptualize and propose new ideas/solutions					
• Can imagine how ideas or alternatives will play out if pursued					
• Can mentally synthesize disconnected/fragmented pieces into a unified whole					
• Can integrate ideas/insights from one field into another (cross-pollination)					
Motivational Skills					
• Can establish rapport through conversation and interpersonal interaction					
• Can convey optimism in facing challenges or setbacks					
• Can coach, mentor, and act as a role model in influencing the performance of others					
• Can recognize and acknowledge the contributions of others					
• Can tolerate mistakes in self and others					
Communication Skills					
• Can use empathic listening strategies					
• Can write clearly, cogently, and persuasively					
• Can prepare and deliver effective speeches, based on purpose and audience					
• Can use technology and audio/visual aids to good advantage					
Team-Building Skills					
• Can encourage independent thinking in others					
• Can solicit input and involve others in decision making					

Categories and Skill Sets	Rating				
	NA	1	2	3	4
Team-Building Skills, continued					
• Can facilitate open communication among team members					
• Can support learning opportunities for team					
• Can give positive feedback and address concerns/issues before serious problems emerge					
Conflict Resolution Skills					
• Can manage conflict appropriately					
• Can use different techniques such as avoidance, accommodation, and collaboration to resolve or mitigate conflictive situations					
• Can promote win-win resolutions					
Decision-Making Skills					
• Can use appropriate decision-making models as needed					
• Can employ intuitive judgment in making choices					
• Can calculate risks and weigh consequences					
• Can allow for midcourse corrections in decisions made					
• Can accept responsibility for failure as well as for success					
Strategic Planning Skills					
• Can assess gaps and needs					
• Can delineate goals, objectives, outcomes, and criteria for success					
• Can identify actions, timelines, and resource needs to support implementation					
• Can select or design evaluation tools to measure progress					
Management and Follow-Through Skills					
• Can select personnel and assign tasks based on skills and expertise					
• Can prioritize tasks based on importance and urgency					
• Can adhere to timelines or other commitments					
• Can deliver products or results with minimal supervision					
• Can secure necessary supports and fiscal resources					
Critical Thinking and Problem-Solving Skills					
• Can accurately define problems					
• Can use brainstorming to generate a variety of solutions					
• Can collect and analyze relevant information and data to verify perceptions					
• Can use logic and reasoning skills with dexterity					

Categories and Skill Sets	Rating				
	NA	1	2	3	4
Advocacy and Public-Relations Skills					
• Can demonstrate passion by combining competence, commitment, and enthusiasm					
• Can organize information and arguments to inform and to engender support for one's platform or agenda					
• Can identify relevant stakeholders and tailor information and delivery channels to their needs					
• Can appear engaged and focused					

Part II

Directions: Check the personality characteristics listed below that best describe you:

- ❑ Introvert
- ❑ Extrovert
- ❑ Motivated by external rewards
- ❑ Motivated by internal desires
- ❑ Passive
- ❑ Proactive
- ❑ Persistent
- ❑ Easily dissuaded or discouraged
- ❑ Gregarious

- ❑ Shy
- ❑ Determined
- ❑ Lackadaisical
- ❑ Rigid
- ❑ Flexible
- ❑ Creative
- ❑ Routinized
- ❑ Perfectionistic

◎ Do you prefer to be (check one):
- ❑ in the spotlight, or
- ❑ behind the scenes in team-oriented activities or projects?

◎ Do you prefer to (check one):
- ❑ work alone,
- ❑ with one other person, or
- ❑ in small or large groups?

◎ When it comes to getting work/assignments completed on time (check one):
- ❑ are you self-directed, or
- ❑ do you need prodding?

Name: _____ Date: _____

Self-Assessment: Success Query

1. What is your definition of or standard for ultimate success in life?

2. To what extent does being a leader in your chosen career and/or vocation constitute an important component of your definition of success? Explain.

3. What academic shortcomings or personality characteristics do you have that might undermine your achievement of success?

4. How can you remediate, circumvent, or override these conditions so that you are able to maximize your potential for achieving success?

Lesson 5
Duke Ellington

Music is how I live, why I live and how I will be remembered.

—Duke Ellington

Instructional Purpose

◎ To practice using the Internet to do biographical research
◎ To map the biographical data against key leadership factors
◎ To understand leadership in the field of music
◎ To compare common elements of modern art and music

Materials

◎ Handout 1.1: Generalizations on Leadership (From Lesson 1)
◎ Handout 4.3: Self-Assessment: Success Query (From Lesson 4)
◎ Handout 5.1: Biographical Chart: Duke Ellington
◎ Teachers' Rap Sheet on Duke Ellington (see Appendix A)

Activities and Instructional Strategies

Part I (1–2 periods)

1. Ask a few students to share their self-assessments about success (Handout 4.3: Self-Assessment: Success Query, which was completed for homework). Compare definitions, strengths, and weaknesses among the group. Construct a class chart of proactive ways for students to improve their leadership skills.

2. Have students conduct Internet research on Duke Ellington to complete Handout 5.1: Biographical Chart: Duke Ellington. Students should read the material at the following websites:
   o Wikipedia (http://en.wikipedia.org/wiki/Duke_Ellington)
   o The Official Site of Jazz Legend Duke Ellington (http://www.dukeellington.com)
   o Biography.com (http://www.biography.com/people/duke-ellington-9286338)
   o The Pulitzer Prizes (http://www.pulitzer.org/biography/1999-Special-Awards-and-Citations)

3. Have the whole class complete a master Biographical Chart by using a white board or overhead projector to compile the information gathered by stu-

DOI:10.4324/9781003233619-15

dents. The teacher may choose to annotate or extend the information in the Biographical Chart by drawing on the data provided in the Teachers' Rap Sheet found in Appendix A. Students should embellish their own charts as the class session unfolds. The teacher should be cognizant of the importance of helping students understand that leadership characteristics vary based on the demands of a field and the talents of individuals within that field.

4. The teacher will engage students in a large-group discussion using the following questions:

   o The talent development process in Duke Ellington may be traced to his early years in Washington, DC. What were the influences on the early Ellington?

   o Ellington is said to have been highly private, sharing his inner self with only a few people, yet he was widely known for his public persona of charm and charisma. Given his introverted personality, how was Ellington able to influence people to join his band, hire him, and help him on his way to becoming the greatest musical genius of the century according to many musicologists?

   o Leadership is comprised of several characteristics. How do these characteristics interact and operate in the life of Duke Ellington?

   o Ellington once said: "The writing and playing of music is a matter of intent. . . . You can't just throw a paint brush against the wall and call whatever happens art. My music fits the tonal personality of the player. I think too strongly in terms of altering my music to fit the performer to be impressed by accidental music. You can't take doodling seriously." What was his point in this statement? How does it offer us a philosophy of his artistry?

   o Ellington was a composer, piano player, and conductor. Which role do you think was he most effective in executing and why do you think so?

   o Ellington created a new idiom for American music that allowed jazz and bebop to be accepted as mainstream during periods of history when other competing forces in music were at work, including rock and roll. How did Ellington's music fit into this evolving pattern of American music? How did the time period in which he worked affect his acceptance as a world-class musician? View "The Artistry of 'Pops': Louis Armstrong at 100," a free video available on iTunes U. In it, both Louis Armstrong and Duke Ellington are discussed by Wynton Marsalis, jazz artist, and Stanley Crouch, jazz historian.

Part II (1–2 periods)

1. Play selections from the Ellington songbook for students. Ask students to free write in their journal responses to the music with respect to the structure, theme, feeling, and images it evokes.

2. Ask students to undertake a study of the relationship between the visual arts and music. Place students in groups of five and ask each group to examine one visual artist to discern how his or her visual artwork depicts musical elements. Use the following artists as the basis for this study and ask students to select three paintings from their chosen artist to analyze:
   o Paul Klee
   o Piet Mondrian
   o George Braque
   o Joan Miró
   o Ivan Kliun

3. As students examine the artwork by the chosen artist, ask them to respond to the following prompts in their journals:
   o Analyze the structure, theme, feelings, and images evoked by the art pieces you are studying.
   o What aspects of the visual arts pieces are similar to Ellington's jazz recordings?
   o What aspects are different?
   o Write a response to the art pieces examined. Create a poem, a metaphor, or an artistic statement to capture how the art affects you.

4. Ask students to share their aesthetic responses to both the music and the art. Discuss the artistic elements identified in each.

Part III (1–2 periods)

1. Have students complete the following timeline activity: Duke Ellington exemplified what might be accomplished in a 50-year career. Create a timeline that highlights his top 10 accomplishments. When they are finished, have students share their timelines with others in their group. Ask 3–5 students to share their timelines with the class and defend their choices.

2. Ask students to examine the generalizations on leadership for this unit. They should select one and apply it to the life of Duke Ellington in a persuasive essay of 250 words.

Assessment

The teacher should check to see that each student has completed the Biographical Chart on Duke Ellington and include it in the student's portfolio. The teacher should also verify that the journal entries in Part II have been completed. Use the journal entries and the discussion of artistic elements to gauge student understanding of aesthetic principles of modern art and music. The teacher should also ensure that the 250-word persuasive essay assigned in Part III has been completed.

Homework

Some of each part of the activities included above could be assigned as homework at different stages of this lesson. Students are assigned responsibility for completing Handout 6.1: Biographical Chart: Pablo Picasso in preparation for the next class period. The four sites that students should be directed to for conducting this research are as follows:

◎ Pablo Picasso Biography (http://pablo-picasso.paintings.name/biography)
◎ Biography.com (http://www.biography.com/people/pablo-picasso-9440021)
◎ Pablo Picasso Paintings, Quotes and Biography (http://www.pablopicasso.org)
◎ Pablo Picasso (YouTube video made by a student; http://www.youtube.com/watch?v=_fNvBJAJw4s)

Extensions

The following ideas are offered as substitutions for parts of the above lesson or as extensions for this lesson focusing on Duke Ellington.

◎ Have students listen to several recordings of Ellington's works as a composer. What can be said about his style?
◎ Encourage students to read a full biography on Ellington. What new insights does it provide about his character?
◎ Have students read an account of the Jazz Age and the Harlem Renaissance. Ask: What contributions to all art forms, including the visual arts, poetry, literature, and music, were made during that period? Situate Ellington's contribution to music within that time period. Have students prepare a creative product that displays their findings.

Biographical Chart: Duke Ellington

Full Name: _____

Lifespan: _____

Early Family Background and Created Family Structure

_____

_____

_____

Personality Characteristics and Areas of Aptitude, Talent, and Interest

_____

_____

_____

Major Career/Professional Events and Accomplishments

_____

_____

_____

Personal Life Themes/Beliefs

_____

_____

_____

Selected Quotations

_____

_____

_____

Awards and Recognition

_____

_____

_____

_____

Lesson 6
Pablo Picasso

Every act of creation is first an act of destruction.

—Pablo Picasso

Instructional Purpose

- ◎ To practice using the Internet to do biographical research
- ◎ To map biographical data against key leadership factors
- ◎ To demonstrate understanding of Picasso's vision for what art might be

Materials Needed

- ◎ Handout 6.1: Biographical Chart: Pablo Picasso
- ◎ Teachers' Rap Sheet on Pablo Picasso (see Appendix A)

Activities and Instructional Strategies

Part I (1 period)

1. The teacher will check to see that students have completed their Biographical Chart for Pablo Picasso.
2. The teacher will then have the whole class complete a master Biographical Chart on Picasso using a white board or overhead projector to compile the information gathered by students. Ask: What did you discover about Picasso's early family background and created family structure? What did you discover about his education? Follow this format until the chart has been completed. The teacher may choose to annotate or extend the information in the Biographical Chart by drawing on the data provided in the Teachers' Rap Sheet found in Appendix A.
3. The teacher should conclude this part of the lesson by pointing out that Duke Ellington and Pablo Picasso were contemporaries. Although Picasso was 18 years older, they died within a year of one another. Picasso was European and lived in Paris for most of his life; Ellington was American and lived in New York City. Ask students to compare and contrast the lives and times of these two leaders.

Part II (1 period)

1. The teacher will engage students in a large-group discussion using the following questions as prompts:

DOI:10.4324/9781003233619-16

o In what ways was Pablo Picasso a leader?

o To what extent did time, place, and circumstances impact his ability to become a leader?

o How would you describe the vision that Picasso brought to the visual arts field? What innovations did he bring to the style of painting? How was Picasso's approach to the visual arts over his lifetime similar to the approach taken by Duke Ellington to his career in music? In what ways did they differ?

o What personal characteristics contributed to Picasso's success as an artist?

o What evidence is there of both initiative and risk taking in Picasso's profile?

o What obstacles did Picasso overcome in his lifetime? Why do you think his political leanings were communistic?

o What do you see as Picasso's lasting impact and contributions in the visual arts? Many art critics believe Picasso was the greatest painter of the 20th century. Do you agree with this assessment? How do you think changes in mass media (e.g., rise of television) that occurred during his lifetime influenced the level of renown and popularity he achieved?

o Picasso said: "Art is a lie that makes us realize the truth." Ask: What does he mean by this statement? Is one style of painting more of a lie than another (e.g., Is cubism more dishonest than classicism, romanticism, or realism?)? (The teacher may have to have some examples of different artistic styles for students to examine. A Norman Rockwell picture would make a good basis for comparison.)

Part III (1 period)

1. The generalization noting that leadership requires vision is an important one for students to understand. Ask: How was Picasso an art visionary in respect to form, theme, subject matter, and use of elements such as perspective, color, and mood?

2. Ask students to select (or you may choose for them) three paintings representing three distinct periods in Picasso's career: his Blue Period, his Rose Period, and his Cubist Period. Have them compare and contrast the styles of these paintings, demonstrate how each period was evolutionary in Picasso's thinking, and explain how each of these periods contributed to the field of art as a whole. Use the following template to record responses on the white board or overhead projector.

Periods	Picture Selected	Style Characteristics	Nature of Evolution	Contribution to Art
Blue				
Rose				
Cubist				

3. Have students create a concept map that demonstrates Picasso's contributions to painting.

Part IV (1 period)

1. The teacher will allow 10–15 minutes for students to complete their journals using some or all of the following questions as prompts:

   o What did you learn from the biographical study of Pablo Picasso that is useful or interesting in your understanding of leadership?

   o In what ways is Pablo Picasso a role model for you and/or other aspiring artists? Are there facets of Picasso's personality or behavior that you dislike or disdain?

   o You have now looked at two leaders in the arts (Ellington and Picasso). In what ways is leadership in the arts like leadership in the sciences? In what ways is it different?

   o Picasso said: "Every child is an artist. The problem is how to remain an artist once he grows up." What did he mean by this? In what ways are you an artist? What can you do to enhance your artistic ability?

2. Ask for some volunteers to share their responses and discuss the questions as a whole class.

Assessment

The teacher should check to see that each student has completed the Biographical Chart on Pablo Picasso. Informally, the teacher should assess the quality of the discussions held and the students' aptness of responses to the questions.

Homework

Students are assigned responsibility for completing Handout 7.1: Biographical Chart: Emily Dickinson in preparation for the next class period. The four sites that students should be directed to for conducting this research are as follows:

   ◎ Wikipedia (http://en.wikipedia.org/wiki/Emily_Dickinson)

   ◎ Biography.com (http://www.biography.com/people/emily-dickinson-92 74190)

◎ Emily Dickinson Online (http://www.emilydickinsononline.org/1.html)
◎ Emily Dickinson: The Poetry Foundation (http://www.poetryfoundation. org/bio/emily-dickinson)

Extensions

The following ideas are offered as substitutions for parts of the above lesson or as extensions for this lesson focusing on Pablo Picasso.

◎ Have students critique the YouTube video made by a student (referenced in the Homework section of Lesson 5 that is part of the student research on Picasso). Have them work in small groups to create their own video or web page targeted to middle school students.

◎ Have students read *Pablo Picasso* by Tim McNeese (from The Great Hispanic Heritage collection). Have them write an essay expanding on Picasso's legacy as a result of their reading and have them make a personal assessment as to the impact of this legacy on the generation of artists that will come from their ranks in the next few decades. What aspects of his work can they relate to? What aspects seem passé?

◎ Have students examine the work of Picasso during his Blue Period. What characterized the art of this period? How does it relate to his life as an artist at that time? Describe the themes and subject matter of one painting from this period.

◎ Have students study Picasso's most famous painting, *Guernica*. It is a depiction of the Spanish Civil War and has become the artistic symbol most associated with that event. Ask: What aspects of the painting allow us to understand the horror Picasso felt about the event? Have students comment on how art can provide support for social causes.

Handout 6.1

Biographical Chart: Pablo Picasso

Full Name: _____

Lifespan: _____

Early Family Background and Created Family Structure

_____

_____

_____

Personality Characteristics and Areas of Aptitude, Talent, and Interest

_____

_____

_____

Major Career/Professional Events and Accomplishments

_____

_____

_____

Personal Life Themes/Beliefs

_____

_____

_____

Selected Quotations

_____

_____

_____

Awards and Recognition

_____

_____

_____

Lesson 7
Emily Dickinson

If I read a book and it makes my whole body so cold no fire can ever warm me, I know that is poetry. If I feel physically as if the top of my head were taken off, I know that is poetry. These are the only ways I know. Is there any other way?

—Emily Dickinson

Instructional Purpose

◎ To practice using the Internet to do biographical research
◎ To map biographical data against key leadership factors
◎ To analyze leadership factors found in the work of Emily Dickinson

Materials Needed

◎ Chart paper
◎ Markers
◎ Handout 1.1: Generalizations About Leadership (from Lesson 1)
◎ Handout 7.1: Biographical Chart: Emily Dickinson
◎ Teachers' Rap Sheet on Emily Dickinson (see Appendix A)

Activities and Instructional Strategies

Part I (1–2 class periods)

1. The teacher will have the whole class complete a master Biographical Chart on Emily Dickinson, based on the information students found from completing their prior homework assignment research. This should be done using a white board or overhead projector. Again, the teacher should use questioning techniques to gather the data needed to complete a master chart. The teacher may choose to annotate the information collected by drawing on the Teachers' Rap Sheet for Dickinson if students have failed to grasp and/or record important pieces of biographical information.

2. Ask students to comment on the most critical events in Dickinson's life and explain why they were so important.

Part II (1 period)

1. The teacher will engage students in a large-group discussion using the following questions:

DOI:10.4324/9781003233619-17

o In what ways was Emily Dickinson a leader?

o If you were to cite her major strengths as a literary leader, what would they be? What is your evidence?

o What qualities made her able to accomplish her writing at a time when few women had such freedom in society?

o What experiences did she have in her early life that contributed to her leadership capacity?

o Emily Dickinson was not a conventional leader yet she influenced poets for the next century with her original form and treatment of key themes. How can we consider someone a leader who had no influence during her lifetime?

o How does she embody the capacity to have vision and take risks to achieve it?

o What does she mean by the stanza: "I dwell in Possibility—A fairer House than Prose—More numerous of Windows—Superior—for Doors—"?

o What were the most powerful influences on Emily in her development as a leader of poetry? Cite evidence to support your perspective.

Part III (1 period)

1. Ask students to use Handout 1.1: Generalizations About Leadership to discuss how the unit generalizations relate to the life of Emily Dickinson. Have the students work in dyads for 15 minutes.

2. Ask students to select one of the following quotes by Emily and write a paragraph describing what she means and how it relates to the generalizations about leadership. Give students 20 minutes to compose their response. Choose one:

   o "Have I said it true? That's what I want to do—say it true."

   o "Hope is the thing with feathers—That perches in the soul—And sings the tune without the words—And never stops—at all—"

   o "My friends are my estate."

3. Ask 5–6 students to read their responses aloud to the class. Discuss each quote with respect to its meaning and significance in illuminating Dickinson's life. How does each quote demonstrate one of the generalizations about leadership?

4. Have students put their writing in their portfolios.

Part IV (1 period)

1. Ask students to write to the following prompt in their journal (15 minutes): To what extent did Dickinson use adversity in her personal life to make a contribution to poetry? Reflect on your understanding of the major events in her life to respond.

2. Discuss the following prompt with the whole class: What is the role of adversity in motivating people to perform tasks beyond their seeming capabilities? What other figures in history might fit this profile as well?

Assessment

The teacher should check to see that each student has completed the Biographical Chart on Emily Dickinson. The teacher may wish to collect the written statements on generalizations to ensure student understanding of the abstract ideas and verify that the journal entries have also been completed.

Homework

Students are assigned responsibility for completing Handout 8.1: Biographical Chart: Nelson Mandela in preparation for the next class period. The three sites that students should be directed to for conducting this research are as follows:

◎ Wikipedia (http://en.wikipedia.org/wiki/Nelson_Mandela)
◎ Nelson Mandela Centre of Memory (http://www.nelsonmandela.org)
◎ Nelson Mandela Biography (http://www.nobelprize.org/nobel_prizes/peace/laureates/1993/mandela-bio.html)

Extensions

The following ideas are offered as substitutions for parts of the above lesson or as extensions for this lesson focusing on Emily Dickinson.

◎ Ask students to choose a biography of Emily Dickinson to read. Have them develop an argument for her inclusion in the American pantheon of eminent people.

◎ Have students choose one of the other generalizations about leadership (one they did not write about in Part III of the lesson) and argue that Emily exemplified it in some way.

◎ Have students consider the life of one of the following authors who lived at the same time as Emily, using their Internet research methods to learn more about the woman's life. How was her life similar yet different from that of Emily Dickinson? Ask students to prepare a poster to illustrate their points. Choose one:

   o Charlotte Brontë

- o Emily Brontë
- o Jane Austen

◎ The following poem may speak volumes about the feelings of Emily Dickinson as she made life choices. Have students read it and comment on how it relates to her life in an essay of 300 words.

> How happy is the little Stone
> That rambles in the Road alone,
> And doesn't care about Careers,
> And Exigencies never fears—
> Whose Coat of elemental Brown
> A passing Universe put on;
> And independent as the Sun,
> Associates or glows alone,
> Fulfilling absolute Decree
> In casual simplicity—

◎ Have students view the DVD of *The Belle of Amherst*, a one-person play starring Julie Harris, and ask them to assess how the film augments their understanding of the life of Emily Dickinson and her legacy as a poetess.

Biographical Chart: Emily Dickinson

Full Name: _____

Lifespan: _____

Early Family Background and Created Family Structure

_____

_____

_____

Personality Characteristics and Areas of Aptitude, Talent, and Interest

_____

_____

_____

Major Career/Professional Events and Accomplishments

_____

_____

_____

Personal Life Themes/Beliefs

_____

_____

_____

Selected Quotations

_____

_____

_____

Awards and Recognition

_____

_____

_____

Lesson 8
Nelson Mandela

During my lifetime I have dedicated myself to the struggle of the African people. I have fought against white domination, and I have fought against black domination. I have cherished the ideal of a democratic and free society in which all persons live together in harmony and with equal opportunities. It is an ideal which I hope to live for and to achieve. But if needs be, it is an ideal for which I am prepared to die.

—Nelson Mandela

Instructional Purpose

◎ To practice using the Internet to conduct biographical research
◎ To map biographical data against key leadership factors
◎ To enhance understanding of adversity in leadership

Materials

◎ Handout 8.1: Biographical Chart: Nelson Mandela
◎ Handout 8.2: Selected Generalizations on Leadership
◎ Teachers' Rap Sheet on Nelson Mandela (see Appendix A)

Activities and Instructional Strategies

Part I (2–3 periods)

1. Ask students to meet in their groups and discuss their homework findings on Nelson Mandela. The teacher will then have the whole class complete a master Biographical Chart on Nelson Mandela using a white board or overhead projector to compile the information gathered by students.
2. Share the following with students: Mandela was elected President of South Africa at the age of 75. Nevertheless, he was capable of accomplishing a number of social reforms. Select one of these reforms and determine its importance and impact on South Africa today. Use the Internet to locate recent sources to help your work. You may work in teams of two to come up with your findings.
3. After the teams have conducted their research, ask a few to discuss the impact of some of Mandela's reforms. Once students have shared their findings, ask:
   o What aspects of Nelson Mandela's personality and character allowed him to emerge as a leader in South Africa?

DOI:10.4324/9781003233619-18

- How does the role of adversity in his life affect his greatness today?
- Nelson Mandela had a big vision for South Africa. What aspects of that vision have been realized? Which ones have not been?
- What is apartheid, and how did it impact the life of Blacks in South Africa?
- What problems did Mandela confront during his presidency? How did he resolve them?

4. Tell students: Mandela is now in his 90s yet still exerts influence worldwide and is perceived as a role model for freedom. Based on your readings about him, what impact has he had on you? Write an entry in your journal responding to that question.
5. After 15 minutes, ask 3–5 students to share their responses with the class.

Part II (1–2 periods)

1. Use Handout 8.2: Selected Generalizations on Leadership to discuss how Mandela's life exemplifies each of them. Ask students to provide evidence from their research to support their point of view. Have students complete the handout individually and then discuss their responses as a group.
2. The teacher should discuss the students' findings, emphasizing the importance of key facets of political leadership.

Assessment

The teacher should check to see that each student has completed the Biographical Chart on Nelson Mandela, Handout 8.2, and the journal entry and include them in the student's portfolio. Ensure that students are making correct inferences from the material provided on Mandela to their work on generalizations about political leadership.

Homework

Have students prepare for their presentations on the self-directed project on leadership.

Extensions

The following ideas are offered as substitutions for parts of the above lesson or as extensions for this lesson focusing on Nelson Mandela.

- Have students select and read one of the biographies available on Nelson Mandela. Ask students to answer the following questions in a written form of their choice (e.g., poem, essay, play):

- o How did Mandela view himself as a leader?
- o What were his attributes that allowed him to captivate others?
- o What were the early signs that Mandela was highly capable of leadership?
- o What role did family play in his life?
- o What do you think he considers to be his greatest accomplishment?
- o What will his legacy be? Write his epitaph.

◎ Have students review a few of Mandela's speeches and watch some of his videos. Ask students to think about his rhetorical style and why it works. They should comment on this in a short paper.

◎ Ask students to contrast his role in South Africa with that of his predecessor, F. W. de Klerk, who shared the Nobel Prize with him in 1990. How were the two men similar and different?

Name: _____ Date: _____

Biographical Chart: Nelson Mandela

Full Name: _____

Lifespan: _____

Early Family Background and Created Family Structure

_____

_____

_____

Personality Characteristics and Areas of Aptitude, Talent, and Interest

_____

_____

_____

Major Career/Professional Events and Accomplishments

_____

_____

_____

Personal Life Themes/Beliefs

_____

_____

_____

Selected Quotations

_____

_____

_____

Awards and Recognition

_____

_____

_____

Selected Generalizations on Leadership

Directions: Look at the selected generalizations on leadership. How does each apply to Nelson Mandela?

1. Leadership is based in action and often requires risk taking.

2. Leadership requires perseverance in the face of challenges and hardships.

3. Leadership is highly dependent on the interplay of intellectual abilities, specific aptitudes and skills, and personality factors.

Selected Generalizations on Leadership

Nelson Mandela

Lesson 9
Presentations and Products on Leadership

....

Instructional Purpose

◎ To engage students in an oral presentation on a leader they have studied
◎ To help them internalize the talent development trajectory of leadership studied in the lives of eminent people.

Materials Needed

◎ Relevant equipment (e.g., LCD projector, computer for PowerPoint presentations)
◎ Handout 9.1: Peer Evaluation Form

Activities and Instructional Strategies

This presentation lesson may take 2–4 periods, depending on the size of the class.

1. Ask students to share their presentations and the product they chose to develop to illustrate the life of the eminent person studied during the unit. Students may volunteer for the order of presentation or may draw lots.
2. While presentations are in progress, the rest of the class will rate each student on Handout 9.1: Peer Evaluation Form.
3. Presentations will be 10 minutes in length at maximum, and three questions can be asked from the rest of the group at the end of the presentation. If the teacher would like, student products can be displayed around the room for a special exhibit fair on leadership for parents and other invited guests. The teacher would set his or her own dates for this event and ensure it is advertised well in advance. The top-rated presentations could be given at the exhibit fair.

Assessment

Teachers will assess student projects, using the rubric presented to students in Lesson 1 (see Handout 1.3: Rubric for Student-Directed Project on Leadership).

DOI:10.4324/9781003233619-19

Homework

Prior to the next class, a panel of local leaders should be convened by the teacher to discuss the generalizations about leadership around which the unit is framed and to discuss characteristics of leadership as they see it practiced in their fields. The local group should be 3–5 community leaders representing law, education, business, politics, the world of scientific research, or other fields from which you can find someone to participate. It is often helpful to contact a nearby university or civic agencies to find local leaders. The purpose of the panel is to provide students the opportunity to interview leaders and get their thoughts on the concept of what it means to be a leader today. Send a copy of the unit generalizations ahead of time to the panel members, asking them to be ready to comment on each of them in their view of leadership so they feel versed in the direction you want the discussion to go.

Tell students about the panel and ask them to be thinking about questions they would like to ask that will expand their own understanding of the concept of leadership as it is carried out in different roles and professions in their local community.

Handout 9.1
Peer Evaluation Form

Directions: Please rate each student presenter, using the following scale:
3 = very effective
2 = effective
1 = somewhat effective
N/A = not applicable

	3	2	1
The presentation was well organized.			
The presenter demonstrated a strong knowledge of his or her subject.			
The presentation followed the guiding questions.			
The product developed to represent the leader was creative.			
The presenter engaged the audience effectively through the use of visuals and other techniques.			

What was the best aspect of the presentation?

What could be improved next time?

Share any other comments you have.

Please complete and return this form by the end of class.

Lesson 10
Local Panel of Leaders

....

Instructional Purpose

- ◎ To provide real-world contemporary examples of leadership
- ◎ To provide a comparative analysis of leadership past and present in specific fields

Materials

- ◎ Handout 10.1: Interview Questions

Activities and Instructional Strategies

Part I (1 period)

1. Introduce the panel to the class and ask each panel member to comment on his or her leadership role and how each views the process. Provide the panel members the generalizations that the class has been studying about leadership and ask that they comment on a few of them with respect to their own area of leadership (they should have prepared this in advance).
2. Allow students to ask their questions that they composed for homework or the sample set provided to them in Handout 10.1: Interview Questions so that the panel can respond to student issues and concerns about leadership.
3. Provide a wrap-up to the panel discussion, emphasizing ideas discussed and areas of similarity and difference among the panelists' view of the leadership generalizations the class has been studying.
4. Thank the panel for coming, and be sure to have students write each panelist a thank-you note for his or her time.

Assessment

Have students add the questions they raised and the panelists' responses to their portfolio. Ask students to reflect on the experience by recording in their portfolios what they learned about contemporary leadership from the interviews.

Homework

Students should review the Biographical Charts of each leader studied in the unit.

DOI:10.4324/9781003233619-20

Handout 10.1
Interview Questions

1. What is your leadership role?

2. How did you prepare for the role?

3. What are your major areas of responsibility? What do you do every day to be a leader in your field?

4. What skills of leadership do you possess?

5. How does your field determine who is a leader?

6. What do you think are the most important qualities of leadership and why?

7. What advice do you have for young people on becoming a leader?

8. Who do you most admire as a leader and why?

Lesson 11
Analysis and Synthesis of Leadership

Instructional Purpose

◎ To compare and contrast leadership skills and emphases across the seven leaders studied

◎ To synthesize student understanding about the concept of leadership and the unit's generalizations

Materials Needed

◎ Handout 11.1: Need to Know Board of Essential Questions

◎ Handout 11.2: Comparative Analysis Chart of Leadership

Activities and Instructional Strategies

Part I (1 period)

1. Pass out copies of Handout 11.1: Need to Know Board of Essential Questions and ask students to work on it first individually, then discuss it with a partner, and then discuss it as a whole group. Students should begin to see the commonalities across leadership with respect to skills, actions, and beliefs. Ask: What are the critical skills, actions, and beliefs that strong leaders must hold? Why are they so necessary? Do all of our leaders possess these qualities? Can you comment on how that is so?

Part II (1 period)

1. Pass out copies of Handout 11.2: Comparative Analysis Chart of Leadership and ask students to work in groups of 3–5 to complete the chart. Ask: To what extent are there similarities and differences among the leaders studied with respect to key leadership ideas (generalizations)? To what extent are the differences based on the domain of leadership? Explain.

Part III (1 period)

1. Now that students have analyzed the qualities of great leaders and generalizations about the idea of leadership, they should write a journal entry about the aspect of leadership that they feel is most important for them

DOI:10.4324/9781003233619-21

to develop and why. They may want to describe their career interests in light of this choice.

2. Have students share a few journal entries and discuss what it might take to be a leader in a few areas like science, the arts, and politics. Ask: Why are these areas of leadership valuable today? How do they match up with your aptitudes and interests, your values and beliefs, and your experiences so far in life?

Assessment

Students will add their work from today to their portfolios for teachers to review.

Homework

Students should prepare for the postassessment by reviewing their overall understanding of the concept of leadership that they have studied in this unit. Students should ask themselves: How would I define leadership?

Name: _____ Date: _____

Need to Know Board of Essential Questions

Think about the leaders we have studied in this unit—Robert Ballard, Charles Darwin, Margaret Thatcher, Duke Ellington, Pablo Picasso, Emily Dickinson, and Nelson Mandela. What do they have in common? Answer the question by reflecting on the following aspects of the leadership of each.

1. What do leaders do?

2. What skills do they possess?

3. What do leaders believe?

Name: _____ Date: _____

Comparative Analysis
Chart of Leadership

Complete the following chart in small groups, discussing what aspects of each Biographical Chart would allow you to see the leadership quality noted as strong in the particular person.

Leader	Visionary	Communicator	Risk Taker	Motivator
Ballard				
Darwin				
Thatcher				
Ellington				
Picasso				
Dickinson				
Mandela				

References

McNeese, T. (2006). *Pablo Picasso.* New York, NY: Chelsea House.

National Association for Gifted Children. (2010). *NAGC Pre-K–Grade 12 Gifted Programming Standards: A blueprint for quality gifted education programs.* Washington, DC: Author.

National Governors Association Center for Best Practices, & Council of Chief State School Officers. (2010). *Common Core State Standards for English Language Arts.* Retrieved from http://www.corestandards.org/the-standards

Partnership for 21st Century Skills. (2011). *Overview.* Retrieved from http://www.p21.org/overview/skills-framework

Taba, H. (1962). *Curriculum development: Theory and practice.* New York, NY: Harcourt, Brace.

Yount, L. (2009). *Robert Ballard: Explorer and undersea archaeologist.* New York, NY: Chelsea House.

Part IV
Appendices

Appendix A
Teachers' Rap Sheets

Teachers' Rap Sheet
Robert Ballard

Full Name: Robert Duane Ballard, Ph.D.

Lifespan: June 30, 1942 to Present

Early Family Background and Created Family Structure

◎ Born in Wichita, KS, and grew up in San Diego, CA
◎ Father was an engineer
◎ Has three siblings
◎ 1966: Married Marjorie Jacobsen, his first wife; had two sons together (one died in a car accident)
◎ 1991: Married Barbara Earle, his second wife; had one son and one daughter together

Education

◎ 1965: Graduated from UC Santa Barbara with degrees in chemistry and geology
◎ Was a member of Sigma Alpha Epsilon fraternity
◎ Completed U.S. Army's ROTC program
◎ 1974: Completed a Ph.D. in marine geology and geophysics from the University of Rhode Island; dissertation was on plate tectonics

Personality Characteristics and Areas of Aptitude, Talent, and Interest

◎ Attributes interest in ocean exploration to reading Jules Verne's *Twenty Thousand Leagues Under the Sea* as a child and growing up by the ocean
◎ Heroes were people like Marco Polo, Captain James Cook, and mythical characters out of Jules Verne's novels
◎ Has a fascination with outer space
◎ When called to active military duty while working on his Ph.D., requested to have his commission transferred from the U.S. Army to the U.S. Navy
◎ Has shown strong ability to persuade individuals and organizations to embrace his dreams and projects
◎ Compulsive worker who has been described as an impatient and driven man with vision

Major Career/Professional Events and Accomplishments

◎ Retired from the U.S. Navy as a Commander

◎ 1974: Developed ANGUS (Acoustically Navigated Geological Underwater Survey), a submersible camera that could remain on ocean floor for up to 14 hours and is capable of taking 16,000 pictures in a single lowering

◎ 1975: Began taking part in the search for and study of deep ocean vents

◎ 1985: Led the joint French and American expedition that discovered the *RMS Titanic*

◎ 1985: Surveyed the wreckage of two sunken U.S. nuclear submarines, *USS Scorpion* and *USS Thresher*, on a secret assignment from the Navy

◎ 1989: Headed expedition that discovered the *Bismarck*, a German battleship

◎ 1989: Founded the JASON Project to bring the wonders of the Earth, air, and sea to educational classrooms

◎ 1993: Surveyed wreck of the *RMS Lusitania*

◎ 1997: Founded the Institute for Exploration, where he developed a suite of remotely operated vehicles (ROV HERCULES) created for deep water archaeological excavation to professional standards

◎ 1998: Found the wreck of the *USS Yorktown*, a U.S. aircraft carrier

◎ 2002: Found the wreck of John F. Kennedy's *PT 109*

◎ Has studied evidence of civilization flooded by the Black Sea, contributing to the Black Sea deluge theory

Personal Life Themes/Beliefs

◎ Believes that wrecks he finds should be left undisturbed as graves rather than undergo any salvage operations

◎ Feels it is his duty to popularize his work, specifically citing Carl Sagan and Jacques Cousteau as influences

◎ Believes that life is a series of great adventures—that all those journeys begin with a dream

◎ Core values include the value of discipline and teamwork and the importance of loyalty and honesty

◎ Has a resolve to discover the unknown in the undersea world

Selected Quotations

◎ "We came around the corner and it was in my view port. There was this wall of steel. Like the slab in 2001, like the walls of Troy at night. It was just big, the end of the universe. It just was there as a statement. We came in and I just looked out of my window—I had to look up—because the Titanic shot up a hundred and some feet above me. I'm down at the very keel, and I just went 'My God.'"

◎ "I'm not so worried about [global] warming, because that is going to happen, and it's happening. I'm more worried about disease, I'm more worried about pandemics. I'm more worried about that than the sea level rising."

◎ "Forever may it remain that way. And may God bless these now-found souls." (On preserving the Titanic wreck site as a grave)

◎ "I would not let an adult drive my robot. You don't have enough gaming experience. But I will let a kid with no license take control of my vehicle system." (On his innovative underwater research devices)

◎ "Everything I'm going to present to you was not in my textbooks when I went to school . . . not even in my college textbooks. I'm a geophysicist, and [in] all my Earth science books when I was a student—I had to give the wrong answer to get an A."

Awards and Recognition

◎ 1987: Named *Discover Magazine*'s Scientist of the Year
◎ 1988: Received honorary doctorate by University of Bath
◎ 1988: Received National Geographic Society Centennial Award
◎ 1990: Received Golden Plate Award from Academy of Achievement
◎ 1990: Received American Geological Institute Award
◎ 1990: Received Westinghouse American Association for the Advancement of Science Award
◎ 1992: Received United States Navy Robert Dexter Award for Scientific Achievement
◎ 1994: Received Kilby International Award
◎ 1996: Received Hubbard Medal from National Geographic Society
◎ 2002: Received Caird Medal from National Maritime Institute
◎ 2003: Received National Endowment for the Humanities Medal
◎ 2004: Received Geological Society of American Public Service Award
◎ 2006: Received Distinguished Achievement Award from the Society of Exploration Geophysicists
◎ 2009: Received Lifetime Achievement Award from the National Marine Sanctuary Foundation
◎ Member of NOAA Science Advisory Board
◎ Commissioner on the President's Commission on Ocean Policy
◎ Holds honorary doctoral degrees from at least 16 colleges and universities

Lasting Impact and Contributions

◎ Explorer opening up new fields of both biology and archaeology
◎ Promoter of education and the study of the world's oceans
◎ Helped advance the concept of plate tectonics and mapped much of the Mid-Atlantic Ridge mountain range of the ocean floor
◎ Found some of the most famous shipwrecks in history

◎ Made some of the most important underwater discoveries in the late 20th century in regard to science and exploration

◎ More than 1.7 million students have participated in JASON programs, learning about natural phenomena and viewing live transmissions from JASON robots as they explore the undersea world

◎ Has published more than 60 scientific articles in journals, including *Science, Nature, Earth and Planetary Science Letters*, and *Journal of Geophysical Research*, and numerous popular books and articles, including *National Geographic Magazine*

Teachers' Rap Sheet
Charles Darwin

Full Name: Charles Robert Darwin

Life Span: February 12, 1809–April 19, 1882

Early Family Background and Created Family Structure

◎ Son of Robert Darwin, a society doctor, and Susannah Wedgwood, whose father was a Unitarian pottery industrialist
◎ Grandfather, Erasmus Darwin, was a physician and poet who also dabbled in naturalism
◎ Cared for by his older sisters after his mother died when he was 8
◎ 1839: Married his cousin, Emma Wedgwood
◎ Had 10 children
◎ His oldest daughter, Annie, died of typhoid in 1851 and his youngest son died of scarlet fever in infancy

Education

◎ Educated in English public schools that emphasized classics and considered scientific learning unsuitable; given the nickname "Gas" by his schoolmates for his interest in chemistry
◎ 1825: Studied medicine at Edinburgh University, where he was exposed to the radical scientists and thinkers who were barred from Oxford or Cambridge for views that dissented from the Church of England
◎ 1828: Switched by his father to Christ's College, Cambridge, in preparation for a career in the clergy

Personality Characteristics and Areas of Aptitude, Talent, and Interest

◎ Although fascinated by the natural world and had shown strong scientific inclinations from early childhood, was too disgusted by surgery to pursue a career in medicine
◎ Was a collector of bug species and studied them continuously

Major Career/Professional Events and Accomplishments

◎ 1831: Started the now-famous voyage to South America on the HMS *Beagle*, sailing as a gentleman companion to the aristocratic captain and excited by the opportunity to make naturalistic observations
◎ After a 5-year voyage (18 months of which he spent on board the ship), he returned with full notebooks, fossils, and plenty of questions

- 1837: Became a fellow of the Geological Society
- Published the *Zoology of the Voyage of the H.M.S. Beagle*, helping establish his reputation as a geologist
- 1839: Had formulated his radical theory of natural selection but was afraid to publish the idea due to the religious climate of his time
- 1842: Moved to the secluded village of Downe in Kent, where he eventually became justice of the peace
- 1859: Felt compelled to publish his ideas in *On the Origin of Species by Means of Natural Selection*, after receiving a letter from the English naturalist Alfred Russel Wallace that contained a similar theory
- 1862–1877: Published books about flowers and plants; his studies in botany were always related to, and used to bolster, his theory of evolution
- 1872: Published *The Expression of the Emotions in Man and Animals* to attack the idea that human facial expression is fundamentally different than that of animals
- Although his works generated controversy, Darwin was too ill to participate in conflict in his later years; was protected by a close circle of friends and scientific defenders that included Thomas Huxley and Joseph Hooker

Personal Life Themes/Beliefs

- Held a strong stance against slavery
- 1851: Still believed that God was the lawmaker of the universe despite formulating a theory that left little room for God, but became an atheist after the death of his daughter
- Despite the "social Darwinism" that was inspired by his theory and carried forward by others (a view that charity was bad because it interfered with survival of the fittest), he held humanitarian beliefs throughout his lifetime

Selected Quotations

- "It is not the strongest of the species that survives, nor the most intelligent, but the one most responsive to change."
- "A man who dares to waste one hour of time has not discovered the value of life."
- "I am not apt to follow blindly the lead of other men."
- "Ignorance more frequently begets confidence than does knowledge: it is those who know little, not those who know much, who so positively assert that this or that problem will never be solved by science."
- "As man advances in civilization, and small tribes are united into larger communities, the simplest reason would tell each individual that he ought to extend his social instincts and sympathies to all members of

the same nation, though personally unknown to him. This point being once reached, there is only an artificial barrier to prevent his sympathies extending to the men of all nations and races."

Awards and Recognition
- 1838: Admitted to the prestigious Athenaeum Club
- 1839: Admitted to the Royal Society in 1839
- 1853: Earned the Royal Medal from the Royal Society for his discoveries about barnacles
- 1864: Received the Copley medal from the Royal Society
- 1868: Received the order *Pour le Merite* from the King of Prussia

Lasting Impact and Contributions
- Founded the field of evolutionary biology with a theory of natural selection that is still accepted as valid today

Teachers' Rap Sheet
Margaret Thatcher

Full Name: Margaret Hilda Thatcher

Life Span: October 13, 1925 to Present

Early Family Background and Created Family Structure

◎ Born Margaret Roberts
◎ Father was a grocer in Lincolnshire; grew up in the flat above one store with her sister, Muriel
◎ Early exposure to politics through her father's position in the local council
◎ 1951: Married Denis Thatcher
◎ 1953: Had twins, Carol and Mark

Education

◎ Attended Huntingtower Road Primary School and Grantham Girls' High School, where she became head girl
◎ Won a place at Somerville College of Oxford University to study chemistry; became president of Oxford's Conservative Association

Personality Characteristics and Areas of Aptitude, Talent, and Interest

◎ Extremely tenacious and persistent
◎ Obstinacy and unwillingness to compromise earned her the nickname the "Iron Lady" from the Soviets

Major Career/Professional Events and Accomplishments

◎ 1959: Elected to the House of Commons as a Member of Parliament for Finchley
◎ 1970: Appointed Education Secretary by Prime Minister Edward Heath
◎ 1979, 1983, 1987: Elected Prime Minister of the United Kingdom three times
◎ Had often-controversial policies and led during a time of high unemployment, but became very popular based on how she handled the Falklands War
◎ 1990: Left office after losing the support of her own party

Personal Life Themes/Beliefs

◎ Raised as a Methodist; later became a member of the Church of England

Changing Tomorrow 2, Grades 6–8 © Taylor & Francis Inc.

◎ Had strong belief in personal responsibility, independence, and self-help that motivated her political ideals of small government and capitalism

Selected Quotations

◎ "We want a society where people are free to make choices, to make mistakes, to be generous and compassionate. This is what we mean by a moral society; not a society where the state is responsible for everything, and no one is responsible for the state."

◎ "In politics if you want anything said, ask a man. If you want anything done, ask a woman."

◎ "I love argument, I love debate. I don't expect anyone just to sit there and agree with me, that's not their job."

◎ "What is success? I think it is a mixture of having a flair for the thing that you are doing; knowing that it is not enough, that you have got to have hard work and a certain sense of purpose."

◎ "You may have to fight a battle more than once to win it."

Awards and Recognition

◎ 1970: Appointed a Member of the Order of Merit by the Queen
◎ 1983: Elected a Fellow of the Royal Society
◎ 1991: Awarded the Presidential Medal of Freedom by the United States
◎ 1992: Received a life peerage as the Baroness Thatcher of Kesteven, earning a spot in the House of Lords
◎ 1992: Began celebrating Margaret Thatcher Day in the Falklands
◎ 1995: Appointed a Lady Companion of the Order of the Garter

Lasting Impact and Contributions

◎ Remains the only female Prime Minister of the United Kingdom as well as the longest-running prime minister in the 20th century
◎ Her conservative policies continue to shape the United Kingdom today

Teachers' Rap Sheet
Duke Ellington

Full Name: Edward Kennedy "Duke" Ellington

Life Span: April 29, 1899–May 24, 1974

Early Family Background and Created Family Structure

◎ Parents were both musicians (piano players)
◎ Began taking piano lessons at age 7
◎ Raised in Washington, DC
◎ 1918: Married his high school sweetheart, Edna Thompson
◎ 1919: Had one son Mercer, who also was a musician and business manager for his father
◎ Grandson, Paul Ellington, also went into music and continued the Duke Ellington Orchestra after his death

Education

◎ Attended Garnet Elementary School in Washington, DC.
◎ Dropped out of Armstrong Manual Training School (high school) where he was studying commercial art
◎ Turned down a scholarship to The Pratt Institute to pursue his interest in music

Personality Characteristics and Areas of Aptitude, Talent, and Interest

◎ Early interest and talent for the piano
◎ Enjoyed all forms of music
◎ Loved baseball and worked selling hot dogs in order to watch the Washington Senators
◎ Had an introverted personality; knew how to divert attention from himself and onto the music
◎ Was considered suave, charismatic, and dapper by women, even as a young boy
◎ Managed his bands with humor, charm, and an understanding of individual needs; rarely conducted using a baton
◎ Lived for music as a mode of life expression

Major Career/Professional Events and Accomplishments

◎ 1914: Created the song "Soda Fountain Rag" by ear, because he had not yet learned to read and write music

- 1917–1919: Launched his musical career, painting commercial signs by day and playing piano by night
- Started his first band in 1917
- Maintained popularity by going on the road and doing radio broadcasts during the Depression while many other artists were out of work
- 1927: Began playing a permanent gig at the Cotton Club in New York City, which lasted a decade
- Created music for many of his band members that catered to their individual style, demonstrating his appreciation for individual talents and how they might be expressed
- Became close to Billy Strayhorn, a talented member of the band who also composed and often revised Ellington's work and led the band in his absence; were successful collaborators on many compositions
- Performed both nationally and internationally with his band, yielding him broader exposure and an international reputation
- Composed scores for many films
- Composed more than 3,000 songs during his lifetime
- Considered to be one of the most influential figures in jazz

Personal Life Themes/Beliefs

- Believed in the power of music to affect people
- Was highly focused on the importance of doing serious work in music

Selected Quotations

- "Music is how I live, why I live and how I will be remembered."
- "People do not retire. They are retired by others."
- "A problem is a chance for you to do your best."
- "There are two kinds of worries—those you can do something about and those you can't. Don't spend any time on the latter."
- "The wise musicians are those who play what they can master."
- "Music is the tonal reflection of beauty."

Awards and Recognition

- 1966: Awarded the Grammy Lifetime Achievement Award
- 1969: Awarded Medal of Freedom by President Nixon
- 1971: He received an honorary Ph.D. from the Berklee College of Music
- 1973: Received the Legion of Honor from France, the highest civilian honor given
- 1999: Awarded a Pulitzer Prize (posthumously)
- Received 13 Grammy awards and was inducted into its Hall of Fame

◎ Had the Duke Ellington School of the Arts in Washington, DC, established to provide high-quality arts education for students, named for him
◎ Had many streets and other geographical sites named for him

Lasting Impact and Contributions

◎ Work revolutionized American music, making jazz a respectable idiom
◎ Most responsible for the rise in jazz as an American form of music

Teachers' Rap Sheet
Pablo Picasso

Full Name: Pablo Ruiz y Picasso

Life Span: October 25, 1881–April 8, 1973

Early Family Background and Created Family Structure

- Born in Malaga, Spain, to José Ruiz Blasco and Maria Picasso y Lopez
- Father descended from old, wealthy family in the Provence Leon region and his mother was of Arabic descent
- Father was curator at local museum, as well as professor of art at the School of Arts and Crafts.
- Had two younger sisters, Dolorés and Concepción (whose death was his first tragedy)
- 1891: Entire family moved to La Coruna
- Father took full control of Pablo's education in art; used his influence with newspapers and jury members of art contests to promote Picasso's work
- 1898: Relationship with parents became strained upon quitting his studies
- 1898: Became severely ill with scarlet fever, spending 40 days in quarantine
- 1900: Had originally signed his artworks Pablo Ruiz (after his father), but changed to Picasso (his mother's last name)
- Married twice: Olga Khoklova and then Jacqueline Roque
- Had four children

Education

- Age 5: Attended school in Malaga, Spain, and began learning to make drawings based on simple geometric forms
- Age 7: Began receiving formal artistic training from father in figure drawing and oil painting
- Was not a good student in all subjects and may have had dyslexia
- 1892–1895: Attended the art school Instituto da Guarda in La Coruna, Spain
- 1895–1897: Studied at the art academy La Lonja in Barcelona, Spain
- 1897–1898: Moved to study at Madrid's Royal Academy of Fine Arts; dropped out when school was unable to improve his standards

Personality Characteristics and Areas of Aptitude, Talent, and Interest

◎ Showed a passion for life and a skill for drawing from an early age
◎ Preoccupied with art to the detriment of his classwork
◎ Developed his artistic talent at an extraordinary rate
◎ Early goal was to become a classical painter, but composition was a weak point of his talent
◎ Had a strong imagination
◎ Considered a strong critical thinker; had a unique power to analyze art
◎ Able to emulate the styles and methods of other painters but create paintings that were still original
◎ Was a womanizer and chauvinist
◎ Could be a charmer but also sarcastic and impatient

Major Career/Professional Events and Accomplishments

◎ 1896: First major painting, *The First Communion*, was included in an exhibition in Barcelona (age 15)
◎ 1897: Declared his independence at age 16
◎ 1900: Obtained his first studio in Montmarte, Paris
◎ 1901: Had his first one-man exhibition in Paris
◎ 1901–1904 (Blue Period): Work was characterized by resignation and mourning consisting of downbeat portraits; paintings were done in shades of blue and blue-green
◎ 1904–1906 (Rose Period): Work regains its romantic quality in a series of paintings that are more optimistic in mood and brighter colored, often using reddish and pink tones.
◎ 1906–1907 (Black Period): Refers to the years in which Picasso falls under the influence of African art, on which he bases a series of drawings, paintings, and woodcarvings
◎ 1907–1915 (Cubism Period): Refers to paintings with an artistic style where recognizable objects are fragmented to show all sides of an object at the same time; works became more and more abstract
◎ Created sculpture and prints throughout his long career, making numerous important contributions to both media
◎ 1937: Painted *Guernica*, which was one of his most celebrated paintings; depicted the destruction by bombing of the town of Guernica during the Spanish Civil War
◎ Wrote 300 poems and two plays during one phase of his life

Personal Life Themes/Beliefs

◎ Was a Communist in his political orientation
◎ Avid participant and painter of the Paris nightlife
◎ Believed that one had to work or one would die

◎ Needed to constantly reinvent himself as an artist

Selected Quotations

◎ "I do not seek. I find."
◎ "Everything you can imagine is real."
◎ "Art is the elimination of the unnecessary."
◎ "All children are artists. The problem is how to remain an artist once he grows up."
◎ "Action is the foundational key to all success."
◎ "An idea is a point of departure and no more. As soon as you elaborate it, it becomes transformed by thought."
◎ "Colors, like features, follow the changes of the emotions."
◎ "He can who thinks he can, and he can't who thinks he can't. This is an inexorable, indisputable law."
◎ "I don't believe in accidents. There are only encounters in history. There are no accidents."
◎ "I paint objects as I think them, not as I see them."
◎ "Different themes inevitably require different methods of expression. This does not imply either evolution or progress; it is a matter of following the idea one wants to express and the way in which one expresses it."

Awards and Recognition

◎ Paintings were used to pay his estate taxes and the city of Paris established the Musée Picasso to showcase these works and others from his personal collection
◎ Several of his paintings are among the highest-priced works ever sold; in 2010, *Nude, Green Leaves, and Bust* was sold for $106.5 million at auction
◎ More of his work has been stolen than any other artist
◎ 1962: Received the Lenin Peace Prize

Lasting Impact and Contributions

◎ Was one of the most productive and revolutionary artists in the history of Western painting
◎ Is one of the most celebrated artists of the modern period

Teachers' Rap Sheet
Emily Dickinson

Full Name: Emily Elizabeth Dickinson

Life Span: December 10, 1830–May 15, 1886

Early Family Background and Created Family Structure
- Born in Amherst, MA
- Had an older brother named Austin and a younger sister named Lavinia
- Never married nor left her birth home; cared for her mother until her death
- Paternal grandfather Samuel Dickinson founded Amherst College
- 1813: Samuel Dickinson had the Homestead built, which became Emily's family home
- Father was treasurer of Amherst College for nearly 40 years, served numerous terms as a state legislator, and represented the Hampshire district in Congress
- Father had a strong desire for his children to be educated

Education
- Attended primary school in Amherst, MA
- Attended Amherst Academy for 7 years; considered a bright, capable, and dutiful student
- Attended college at Mt. Holyoke (female seminary) but never graduated
- Returned home after a semester at Mt. Holyoke for multiple reasons, including health and homesickness

Personality Characteristics and Areas of Aptitude, Talent, and Interest
- Loved to read and write
- Loved the piano and the sounds of music
- Trained in botany, she had a passion for flowers and enjoyed creating a garden at the Homestead
- Was a recluse for much of her life, not going out or even meeting with friends in her own home
- Preferred to communicate with letters.
- Had a very introverted personality; was easily hurt and highly sensitive to others' pain and the trauma of death

Major Career/Professional Events and Accomplishments

◎ Had her accomplishments as a poet recognized after her death when her complete volume of poetry was published

◎ Had The Emily Dickinson International Society and an archive named after her

◎ Gained an international reputation as one of America's best poets

Personal Life Themes/Beliefs

◎ Was a highly spiritual human being who worshipped in her own way at home; believed in a God and a higher power and often referred to this belief in her poetry

◎ Loved flowers; would often send a flower with a poem to close friends on a special occasion

◎ Had an unusual overreaction to death, often becoming ill and withdrawn after the death of someone in her close circle

Selected Quotations

◎ "Hope is the thing with feathers—That perches in the soul—And sings the tune without the words—And never stops—at all—"

◎ "If I can stop one heart from breaking, I shall not live in vain; If I can ease one Life the Aching, or cool one Pain, Or help one fainting Robin Unto his nest again I shall not live in Vain."

◎ "I never saw a moor, I never saw the sea; Yet know I how the heather looks, And what a wave must be. I never spoke with God, Nor visited in heaven; Yet certain am I of the spot As if the chart were given."

◎ "If I read a book and it makes my whole body so cold no fire can ever warm me, I know *that* is poetry. If I feel physically as if the top of my head were taken off, I know *that* is poetry. These are the only way I know. Is there any other way?"

◎ "I dwell in Possibility—A fairer House than Prose—More numerous of Windows—Superior—for Doors—"

◎ "There is no Frigate like a Book / To take us Lands away / Nor any Coursers like a Page / Of prancing Poetry—"

◎ "Find ecstasy in life; the mere sense of living is joy enough."

◎ "My friends are my estate."

◎ "Saying nothing . . . sometimes says the most."

Awards and Recognition

◎ Published very few poems during her lifetime; the 1,800 poems found by her sister after her death created a renewed interest in her style and the breadth of her work

- 1950s: reputation had grown as a result of the publication of her complete poems
- Considered the top American female poet of the 19th century
- Awards have all been posthumous; has had biographies published and her work collected for the finest literary anthologies
- One critic noted of her: "Poetry, the Belle of Amherst knew, is that form of communication in which words are never simple equivalents of experience or perception. The words themselves, the words as words, have a life as sounds, as images, as the means for generating a series of associations."

Lasting Impact and Contributions

- Her poetry has been anthologized throughout the world
- Her unique voice has caused many followers to form societies that study her poetry

Teachers' Rap Sheet

Nelson Mandela

Name: Nelson Rolihlahla Mandela

Lifespan: July 18, 1918 to Present

Early Family Background and Created Family Structure

- ◎ Born in Eastern Cape, a province of South Africa
- ◎ Descended from royalty
- ◎ Child of his father's third wife; had around 13 siblings
- ◎ 1958: Married Evelyn Mase
- ◎ Has four children

Education

- ◎ Received a British primary education at local mission school
- ◎ Attended Clarkebury Boarding School
- ◎ Attended Healdtown Wesleyan secondary school
- ◎ 1942: Received a bachelor's degree from University of South Africa
- ◎ Attended University of the Witwatersrand but didn't graduate (left in 1948)

Personality Characteristics and Areas of Aptitude, Talent, and Interest

- ◎ Views armed struggle as a last resort, to be used only when nonviolent means have failed
- ◎ Works toward equality of all races

Major Career/Professional Events and Accomplishments

- ◎ 1943: Joined African Nation Congress; worked under Anton Lembede to enlarge and reform the movement
- ◎ 1962: Arrested and convicted of sabotage; served 27 years in prison
- ◎ 1990: Released from prison; began working for the establishment of democracy and equality in South Africa
- ◎ 1994–1999: Served as President of South Africa

Personal Life Themes/Beliefs

- ◎ Baptized as a Methodist

Selected Quotations

- "We speak here of the challenge of the dichotomies of war and peace, violence and non-violence, racism and human dignity, oppression and repression and liberty and human rights, poverty and freedom from want."
- "When a man is denied the right to live the life he believes in, he has no choice but to become an outlaw."

Awards and Recognition

- 1990: Awarded Lenin Peace Prize
- 1993: Awarded Nobel Peace Prize
- 2001: Became a honorary citizen of Canada
- 2002: Awarded U.S. Presidential Medal of Freedom

Lasting Impact and Contributions

- Has made lasting contributions to human rights and racial equality and integration in South Africa

Appendix B
Annotated Bibliography

Biographic Compendia

Adams, S., Ashe, C., Chrisp, P., Johnson, E., Langley, A., & Weeks, M. (1999). *1000 makers of the millennium*. New York, NY: DK Publishing.

Organized into 10 centuries, the book identifies and provides brief biographies of 1,000 influential people. Many color photographs and illustrations are included. There is a strong contingent of celebrities and sports figures chosen for the late 1900s, which may be a commentary on the times in which we live.

Ashby, R., & Ohrn, D. G. (Eds.). (1995). *Herstory: Women who changed the world*. New York, NY: Viking Press.

This reference book begins with an introductory essay by Gloria Steinem that documents several examples of prejudice against women up through the last half of the 20th century. The book is subdivided into three sections, grouped by time periods: prehistory to 1750; 1750 to 1850; and 1890 to around 1990. The first section contains 21 brief biographies, including Queen Hatshepsut, Sappho, Joan of Arc, Queen Isabella I, and Queen Elizabeth I. Section II contains more than 40 brief biographies including Sacajawea, Sojourner Truth, the Brontë sisters, Clara Barton, Jane Addams, and Beatrix Potter. The third section contains more than 50 brief biographies of women from a wide range of fields. All three sections have introductory essays and are drawn from an international template.

Meadows, J. (1997). *The world's great minds*. London, England: Chancellor Press.

Biographies of 12 great thinkers are presented with supporting information about the times and cultures in which their contributions were embedded. The individuals include Aristotle, Galileo Galilei, William Harvey, Sir Isaac Newton, Antoine Lavoisier, Alexander von Humboldt, Michael Faraday, Charles Darwin, Louis Pasteur, Marie Curie, Sigmund Freud, and Albert Einstein. This text contains many color and black and white photographs and illustrations.

The Editors of Salem Press. (2009). *American heroes* (Vol. 3). Pasadena, CA: The Salem Press.

Sixty-four brief biographies with reference citations are presented alphabetically for American notables whose last names range from Nicklaus to Zacharias. Included are such luminaries as Chester Nimitz, Sandra Day O'Connor, Walter Reed, Jackie Robinson, Eleanor Roosevelt, Sacajawea, and Tecumseh. There are two other volumes of this book that contain brief biographies of leaders included in this curriculum unit. Volume 1 covers heroes whose names range from Aaron to Geronimo. Included in this volume are Jane Addams, Robert Ballard, Clara Barton, Rachel Carson, César Chávez, Walt Disney, Amelia Earhart, Dwight Eisenhower, and Bill Gates. Volume 2 ranges from Gibson to Navratilova and includes Steve Jobs.

Time/CBS News. (1999). *People of the century: One hundred men and women who shaped the last one hundred years.* New York, NY: Simon and Schuster.

Biographical information in the context of brief essays is presented on 100 personalities or representatives of ideas that media sources suggested defined the 20th century. The people selected range from Sigmund Freud, Emmeline Pankhurst, Theodore Roosevelt, and Henry Ford at the beginning of the 1900s, to Oprah Winfrey, Bill Gates, Bart Simpson, and the "Unknown Tiananmen Square Rebel" at the end of the century. Interesting photographs in both color and black and white are interspersed with the text.

Autobiographies and Biographies on Leaders in the Unit

The following readings exemplify the lives and works of the leaders studied in this unit, sometimes told from their own vantage point through autobiography or primary-source material they have written. Most of the entries are biographical, capturing the life of each luminary at key stages if they are still alive or throughout their lives if they are deceased.

Berger, J. (1993). *The success and failure of Picasso* (3rd ed.). New York, NY: Vintage Books.

Browne, J. (1996). *Charles Darwin: Voyaging* (Vol. 1). Princeton, NJ: Princeton University Press.

Browne, J. (2003). *Charles Darwin: The power of place* (Vol. 2). Princeton, NJ: Princeton University Press.

Campbell, J. (2011). *The Iron Lady: Margaret Thatcher, from grocer's daughter to Prime Minister* (Vol. 2). New York, NY: Random House.

Darwin, C. (2008). *The origin of species*. New York, NY: Bantam. (Original work published 1859)

Darwin, C. (1989). *Voyage of the Beagle*. New York, NY: Penguin Books. (Original work published 1839)

Huffington, A. S. (1988). *Picasso: Creator and destroyer*. New York, NY: Simon and Schuster.

Lawrence, A. H. (2001). *Duke Ellington and his world: A biography*. New York, NY: Routledge.

Mandela, N. (1995). *Long walk to freedom: The autobiography of Nelson Mandela*. Boston, MA: Little, Brown.

Sampson, A. (2000). *Mandela: The authorized biography*. New York, NY: Vintage Books.

Sewall, R. B. (1998). *The life of Emily Dickinson*. Cambridge, MA: Harvard University Press.

Tucker, M. (1995). *The Duke Ellington Reader*. New York, NY: Oxford University Press.

Yount, L. (2009) *Robert Ballard: Explorer and undersea archaeologist*. New York, NY: Chelsea House.

Research Literature on Leadership

Bennis, W., & Goldsmith, J. (2010). *Learning to lead: A workbook on becoming a leader* (4th ed.). New York, NY: Basic Books.

This text identifies four characteristics that are wanted from today's leaders (providing purpose, direction, and meaning; building and sustaining trust; purveying hope and optimism; and delivering results) and offers insights and explication to help managers develop into leaders.

Blank, W. (2001). *The 108 skills of natural born leaders*. New York, NY: Amacom.

Starting with the premise that no one is a born leader, this text identifies 108 skills that can be developed to strengthen leadership capabilities in people. Blank differentiates between people who are managers and people who are leaders. He includes a self-assessment inventory that organizes the 108 skills into nine sets: self-awareness, capacity to develop rapport with people, ability to clarify expectations, ability to map the territory to identify the need to lead, ability to chart a course of leadership action, ability to develop others as leaders, ability to build the base to gain commitment, ability to influence others to willingly follow, and ability to create a motivating environment. The last skill he posits is the ability to continually seek renewal.

Bolman, L. G., & Deal, T. E. (2008). *Reframing organizations: Artistry, choice, and leadership* (4th ed.). San Francisco, CA: Jossey-Bass.

The authors offer an interesting lens through which to view the leadership construct. They suggest that effective leadership involves making judgments about the combined use of four leadership frames: (1) structural—the role of tasks and organizational hierarchies (architect); (2) human resources—the role of relationship building (catalyst); (3) political—the role of power distribution (advocate); and (4) symbolic—the role of meaning (prophet). They see leadership as situational and change as involving conflict and loss. Their perspective is drawn from the field of business, and they identify the characteristics of high-performing companies.

Covey, S. R. (2004). *The 7 habits of highly effective people* (Rev. ed.). New York, NY: Simon and Schuster.

This bestseller identifies seven time-honored factors that underscore effective leadership. Covey's synthesis includes (1) being proactive, honoring commitments, and initiating change; (2) developing personal mission statements, setting goals, and identifying desired outcomes; (3) the importance of self-awareness and identity; (4) prioritizing what's important (planning, organizing, time management); (5) win-win relationship-building (character, integrity, trust, cooperation, and honesty); (6) empathic communication (listening and understanding); and (7) creative cooperation (synergy), team-building, and collaboration.

Gardner, H. (2011). *Creating minds: An anatomy of creativity seen through the lives of Freud, Einstein, Picasso, Stravinsky, Eliot, Graham, and Gandhi.* New York, NY: Basic Books.

The author uses the study of seven creative individuals drawn from different domains to offer insights on the construct of creativity. He believes that creativity evolves from the interaction of domains, individuals, and fields and that it is novel problem solving within a domain that ultimately becomes accepted. He discusses the criticality of early support and the Faustian bargain that individuals make in order to rise to the top of their fields.

Hamer, D., & Copeland, P. (1998). *Living with our genes: Why they matter more than you think.* New York, NY: Doubleday Books.

Behavioral aptitudes, personality preferences, and individual temperaments are programmed into our genes, but preference does not mean that the behavior will be actualized. True skill mastery requires practice. This understanding of the developmental dimension of leadership underscores the lessons in this curriculum unit.

Kouzes, J. M., & Posner, B. Z. (1999). *The leadership challenge planner: An action guide to achieving your personal best.* San Francisco, CA: Jossey-Bass.

This clear and insightful text identifies five skill sets that define effective leadership. The authors posit that leaders (1) are pioneers and early adopters of innovation who lead the way by challenging the process and taking risks, (2) inspire a shared vision through dialogue, (3) enable others to act through team-building, (4) model the way through careful planning, and (5) encourage and nurture by feedback, praise, celebration, and rewards.

Mai, R., & Akerson, A. (2003). *The leader as communicator: Strategies and tactics to build loyalty, focus effort, and spark creativity.* New York, NY: Amacom.

This text makes the argument that the primary skill set in effective leadership is related to communication and that leadership communication is about relationship building. It identifies three communication roles for leaders: building community by making meaning, navigating and setting direction, and championing the renewal process. The chapter entitled "Storyteller" relates how the use of stories, anecdotes, and parables can inform and educate as well as inspire.

Nanus, B. (1992). *Visionary leadership.* San Francisco, CA: Jossey-Bass.

This primer on leadership endorses the idea that there are differences between managers and leaders (previously posited by Bennis and Goldsmith) and discusses specific characteristics related to the idea of vision, including that a powerful vision is capable of attracting others, creating meaning, establishing excellence, and forecasting future directions. The author believes that leadership is a mix of judgment (structure, assessment, form, and purpose) and instinct (intuition) and that teaching leadership is important at K–12 levels if the U.S. is to be competitive in the 21st century.

Payne, V. (2001). *The team-building workshop.* New York, NY: Amacom.

This text offers steps, strategies, and exercises in the art of team-building, starting with an understanding of the value of team-building to an organization.

It is designed for individuals who are conducting team-building workshops or sessions. Of particular note is the section on resolving team conflict and the inventory of experiential exercises.

Quick, T. L. (1992). *Successful team building.* New York, NY: Amacom.

This how-to manual for team-building offers helpful chapters on the nature and benefits of a team, including characteristics of effective and ineffective teams, building commitment, dealing with conflict, and group problem solving and decision making.

Simonton, D. K. (1994). *Greatness: Who makes history and why.* New York, NY: Guilford Press.

Using historical research as a basis for exploring the concept of greatness, Simonton offers valuable insights that impact the literature on the construct of leadership. Among the ideas he explores are the role of creativity in leadership; human potential and the development of talent (born or learned or situational); the role of models and mentors in leadership; the importance of personality (self-actualizers, extroversion and introversion); early exposure and learning in a field as predictive of later accomplishment; factors of family, education, stimulation, adversity, and marginality; and the role of motivation and drive.

Wallace, D. B., & Gruber, H. E. (1989). *Creative people at work: Twelve cognitive case studies.* New York, NY: Oxford University Press.

This interesting take on creativity discusses ideas that have salience for the research on leadership. The text is organized around four basic themes: (1) an evolving systems approach (organization of knowledge, purpose, and affect) to understanding the construct of creativity in the domain of work, (2) networks of enterprise, (3) the role of novelty and chance, and (4) personal freedom and social responsibility—the twin tensions of creators/leaders (i.e., moral and ethical leadership).

About the Authors

Joyce VanTassel-Baska, Ed.D., is the Jody and Layton Smith Professor Emerita at The College of William and Mary, where she developed a graduate program and a research and development center in gifted education. Formerly, she initiated and directed the Center for Talent Development at Northwestern University. She has also served as the state director of gifted programs for Illinois, as a regional director of a gifted service center in the Chicago area, as coordinator of gifted programs for the Toledo, OH, public school system, and as a teacher of gifted high school students in English and Latin. Dr. VanTassel-Baska has published widely, including 27 books and more than 500 refereed journal articles, book chapters, and scholarly reports. Her major research interests are the talent development process and effective curricular interventions with the gifted.

Linda D. Avery, Ph.D., managed the Center for Gifted Education at The College of William and Mary upon receiving her doctorate in educational leadership, policy, and planning from that institution in the late 1990s. Previously she helped establish the first gifted education program at the state level in Michigan and helped administer the long-established state program in Illinois. She has authored language arts curriculum materials based on the Integrated Curriculum Model (ICM) and oversaw the preparation of a collection of social studies curriculum units. She has conducted several state and local gifted program evaluation studies over her career and numerous professional development workshops in curriculum development and implementation. She is currently living in Seville, OH.

Common Core
State Standards Alignment

Grade Level	Common Core State Standards
Grade 6 ELA-Literacy	RI.6.1 Cite textual evidence to support analysis of what the text says explicitly as well as inferences drawn from the text.
	RI.6.3 Analyze in detail how a key individual, event, or idea is introduced, illustrated, and elaborated in a text (e.g., through examples or anecdotes).
	RI.6.7 Integrate information presented in different media or formats (e.g., visually, quantitatively) as well as in words to develop a coherent understanding of a topic or issue.
	W.6.4 Produce clear and coherent writing in which the development, organization, and style are appropriate to task, purpose, and audience. (Grade-specific expectations for writing types are defined in standards 1–3 above.)
	W.6.9 Draw evidence from literary or informational texts to support analysis, reflection, and research.
	SL.6.1 Engage effectively in a range of collaborative discussions (one-on-one, in groups, and teacher-led) with diverse partners on grade 6 topics, texts, and issues, building on others' ideas and expressing their own clearly.
Grade 7 ELA-Literacy	RI.7.1 Cite several pieces of textual evidence to support analysis of what the text says explicitly as well as inferences drawn from the text.
	RI.7.3 Analyze the interactions between individuals, events, and ideas in a text (e.g., how ideas influence individuals or events, or how individuals influence ideas or events).
	W.7.4 Produce clear and coherent writing in which the development, organization, and style are appropriate to task, purpose, and audience. (Grade-specific expectations for writing types are defined in standards 1–3 above.)
	W.7.9 Draw evidence from literary or informational texts to support analysis, reflection, and research.
	SL.7.1 Engage effectively in a range of collaborative discussions (one-on-one, in groups, and teacher-led) with diverse partners on grade 7 topics, texts, and issues, building on others' ideas and expressing their own clearly.
Grade 8 ELA-Literacy	RI.8.1 Cite the textual evidence that most strongly supports an analysis of what the text says explicitly as well as inferences drawn from the text.
	RI.8.3 Analyze how a text makes connections among and distinctions between individuals, ideas, or events (e.g., through comparisons, analogies, or categories).
	W.8.4 Produce clear and coherent writing in which the development, organization, and style are appropriate to task, purpose, and audience. (Grade-specific expectations for writing types are defined in standards 1–3 above.)
	W.8.9 Draw evidence from literary or informational texts to support analysis, reflection, and research.
	SL.8.1 Engage effectively in a range of collaborative discussions (one-on-one, in groups, and teacher-led) with diverse partners on grade 8 topics, texts, and issues, building on others' ideas and expressing their own clearly.

Printed and bound by CPI Group (UK) Ltd, Croydon, CR0 4YY

08/06/2025

01896981-0002